Vivienne Rowett

OLD TESTAMENT

General Edit

R.N. Whybr

GENESIS 12–50

GENESIS 12-50

R.W.L. Moberly

Sheffield Academic Press

For Martin, my first Bible teacher,
and Barbara, who is not too sure about the Old Testament

First Published by JSOT Press 1992
Reprinted 1995

Published by Sheffield Academic Press Ltd
Mansion House
19 Kingfield Road
Sheffield, S11 9AS
England

Printed on acid-free paper in Great Britain
by The Cromwell Press
Melksham, Wiltshire

British Library Cataloguing in Publication Data

A catalogue record for this book is available
from the British Library

ISBN 1-85075-371-7

CONTENTS

Contents

ABBREVIATIONS

AB	Anchor Bible
Bib	*Biblica*
BJS	Brown Judaic Studies
BZAW	Beihefte zur *Zeitschrift für die alttestamentliche Wissenschaft*
CBQ	*Catholic Biblical Quarterly*
CBQMS	*Catholic Biblical Quarterly*, Monograph Series
ET	English Translation
FOTL	The Forms of the Old Testament Literature
FRLANT	Forschungen zur Religion und Literatur des Alten und Neuen Testaments
HKAT	Handkommentar zum Alten Testament
HSM	Harvard Semitic Monographs
IBC	Interpretation: A Bible Commentary
ICC	International Critical Commentary
IDB	*Interpreter's Dictionary of the Bible*
IDBSup	*IDB*, Supplementary Volume
JBL	*Journal of Biblical Literature*
JJS	*Journal of Jewish Studies*
JSOT	*Journal for the Study of the Old Testament*
JSOTSup	*Journal for the Study of the Old Testament*, Supplement Series
OTL	Old Testament Library
TOTC	Tyndale Old Testament Commentaries
VT	*Vetus Testamentum*
VTSup	*Vetus Testamentum*, Supplements
WBC	Word Biblical Commentary
WMANT	Wissenschaftliche Monographien zum Alten und Neuen Testament

1

HOW SHOULD
WE READ THE TEXT?

THE STORIES OF THE PATRIARCHS are among the most
famous and memorable of all the stories in the Bible. Abraham
is called by God to leave home and family, waits many years
for a son and then is called to sacrifice that son to God; Jacob
sees a ladder up to heaven at Bethel and wrestles with a mysterious adversary at the ford of the Jabbok; Joseph dreams
prophetic dreams, rises to power in Egypt after being sold as a
slave by his brothers, and rescues his family in time of famine.
Although these stories are generally less well known now than
they used to be, they are not only deeply embedded in the culture of Western civilization, but they also retain their ability
powerfully to capture the imagination of the modern reader
who encounters them.

Despite, or perhaps even because of, their great imaginative
power, the best way to read these stories in the context of
modern biblical scholarship has become problematic.
Particularly at the present time, the whole question of method
and approach in reading the Old Testament has become controversial, and nowhere are the problems more acute than
with the stories of the patriarchs.

The General Context of Debate

On the one hand, the predominant approach to Genesis 12–50
in modern times has been that of the ancient historian. The
primary concern has been to analyze the text in the way that

ancient historians analyze any ancient narrative text. Thus questions of authorship, date and context of composition, possible underlying sources and traditions, genre and historical worth of content, editorial bias, and other similar matters have largely filled works of scholarship. Although recognition of the imaginative power of the stories has not been lacking, it has often been doubtful whether this recognition has made any genuine difference to the way the text has been studied; that is, the significant scholarly agenda has been that of the ancient historian, and the imaginative force of the stories has tended to function as a matter for comment in passing rather than as presenting an important agenda for study in its own right. Nonetheless, the gains from this historical agenda have been considerable, and there has emerged a much clearer understanding of the patriarchal stories as ancient texts in a way which greatly enhances their interest for most readers.

On the other hand, in recent years there has been a growing reaction to the predominance of the historian's agenda, precisely because it leaves important dimensions of the text, in particular its extraordinary imaginative power, largely or wholly untouched. In general terms, the move by some scholars has been to the agenda of literature rather than that of history. Literary approaches have been extremely diverse, but there has generally been a concern to try to analyze how and why it is that these stories make their memorable impact. Thus questions of storytelling technique (stance of narrator, plot, structure, characterization, recurrent and variant motifs, creation and resolution of suspense, etc.) have come to the fore. Interest in the biblical writer, if present at all, now tends to be less to do with what may be learned about him as a historical figure (date, context, reason for writing, etc.) than in what may be learnt about his skills as a literary artist.

One of the less helpful features of some modern debate is the suggestion, either explicit or implicit, that these two different approaches are somehow incompatible. One can work through the fine historical commentary on Genesis of, say, C. Westermann, and have little greater awareness or understanding of the imaginative power of the stories. Alternatively, in one of the outstanding works of literary study,

M. Sternberg's *Poetics of Biblical Narrative*, there is a clear statement of principle that historical and literary approaches are not mutually exclusive. But in his practice Sternberg consistently opts for literary rather than historical explanations of puzzles in the text, even when there is a reasonable *prima facie* case for a historical explanation; the only historical insight that is consistently utilized is a knowledge of Hebrew as an ancient language. There is, however, no instrinsic reason why one should have to choose between historical and literary approaches, or why one should not opt for 'both–and', rather than 'either–or'. Nonetheless, the practical tendency of many scholars to opt for 'either–or' can make it difficult for the student to see how the varying approaches to the text may best be combined with each other.

Although discussions of approaches to the text are often couched in terms of the historical and the literary as the only two alternatives, it is important not to forget what might perhaps best be called 'committed' approaches, which relate the biblical text to the issues of life today and read the text explicitly in the light of contemporary concerns. Of these, the one that has probably attracted most attention in recent debate is feminism (which of course overlaps in varying ways with historical and literary approaches; for a literary-feminist approach, see e.g. Phyllis Trible's reading of the story of Hagar in her *Texts of Terror*). It is important not to forget, however, that the classic Christian approach to the Old Testament is a 'committed' approach. Indeed, it is most probably for religious and theological reasons—because these stories are part of Scripture—that most people still today want to study the stories in the first place. This is not to deny that the stories may legitimutely be studied from historical or other perspectives without regard to their continuing religious value; it is simply that in practice the religious reason for reading tends to be predominant.

But what difference does a religious approach make? In the first place, it is clear that a religious approach is a *motive* rather than a *method*. It may well be that religious motives can be satisfied through literary and historical methods. And this assumption seems to characterize most modern

Old Testament studies and commentaries.

Secondly, however, it should be noted that for most of the last two thousand years, until relatively recent times, it has been generally supposed that a religious approach did bring with it a method of its own (just as a committed feminist approach self-consciously develops its own methodology). For example, the assumption that the text may have a meaning other than solely that of its face value, and that special methods are in order to dig out these further meanings, has characterized the vast majority of pre-modern Old Testament studies, and still survives among sophisticated modern commentators. Perhaps the best known forms of this approach are typology and allegory. It is unfortunate that, because both typology and allegory so easily lend themselves to far-fetched interpretations of the text, and have so often been used badly, they have fallen into general disrepute; for when used well they may in fact be valuable means of applying the text to the life of the community of faith (for a sophisticated modern typology, see von Rad's treatment of Gen. 22 at the end of Chapter 6).

Another way of posing the issue of the difference that a religious approach may make is to ask whether the Bible should be interpreted 'like any other book'—as the issue was put by the distinguished Victorian classicist, Benjamin Jowett, in his famous essay, 'On the Interpretation of Scripture', in the 1860 volume of *Essays and Reviews*. Jowett was objecting to the enormous diversity of conflicting interpretations that attach to Scripture in a way he felt to be uncharacteristic of any other book, and he argued that biblical interpretation could be greatly improved if the Bible was read like any other book and the interpreter concentrated solely on recovering the original sense of Scripture, with its history of later interpretations cut away (i.e. Jowett's statement was programmatic for the historical approach to Scripture that has predominated ever since). The response to Jowett's proposal, at least from the point of view of Christian theology, must be both yes and no. Yes, in the sense that the Bible was written in known ancient languages and according to the known (or generally able to be inferred) conventions of ancient literature. No, in the sense that the material has a certain unique content which has always been integrally related to the continuing life of communities of faith. This latter point affects the material in at least two ways. First, it means that the material itself has acquired something of an internal history through having new insights incorporated into it over a period of time prior to the fixation of the text in its canonical form; this makes the quest for its 'original' meaning peculiarly problematic. Secondly, it means that the material is read in a way unlike that in which any other book is read—it is both constantly read and expounded in public gatherings of Christians and Jews, and it is constantly re-read and pondered in private devotional reading. One assumption underlying this public and private use of the material as Scripture is that it is able to inform and mould the conscience and so shape the beliefs, values and practices of believers. However much other books may be valued, they are not read in this same kind of privileged way. It is important, therefore, that in any account of an Old Testament book, or portion of a book, such as Genesis 12–50, one should be aware of the issues raised by the material's function as Scripture for those who approach it from the perspective of its continuing religious significance.

Part of the difficulty in deciding how best to approach the patriarchal narratives lies in the possible assumption that one should be able to resolve the issue simply by looking at the text and at the different methods of interpretation available. For one indispensable element must in fact be the interests and concerns of the reader. That is to say, different readers quite legitimately have different questions and concerns in mind when they approach the biblical text (for an entertaining account of this from a Jewish perspective, see J. Magonet, *A Rabbi's Bible*). To the person who is interested in historical questions, explanation of the imaginative power of the text may be of limited significance; and vice versa. In short, *how* we read the text will vary according to *why* we read the text. The search for *one* 'correct' reading is largely illusory, and one must accept a plurality of interpretations corresponding to the plurality of legitimate agendas with which the text may be approached. This does not mean that 'anything goes', for there will always be criteria to distinguish better readings from worse readings. The point is simply that the question of better and worse interpretations cannot be decided in isolation from a consideration of the assumptions and priorities held as a consensus view by the group to which the interpreter belongs.

One of the things that may make biblical study difficult for many students is precisely the uncertainty as to which interpretative group they belong. A student from a Church background may have been taught in that context to read the text in one kind of way (e.g. devotionally and practically); when that student comes to university, he or she may be encouraged to read the text in a different kind of way (e.g. with a critical analysis unrelated to devotional and practical concerns). Particularly if, as is often the case, people in each of those contexts say, or at least imply, that their way is the only proper way to read the text, questions of identity may be acute for the student. Yet they may never be explicitly addressed if discussion is restricted to the biblical text and different interpretative methods, and little or no attention is given to the life situation of all concerned. Nonetheless, such wider concerns should never be an excuse for not paying careful attention to the specific features of the biblical text.

Finding a Starting-Point within the Text

How, then, might one in practice approach the patriarchal narratives? I suggest that one good way is via reflection on the traditional ascription of Genesis 12–50 (along with everything else in the Pentateuch) to Moses. The significance of this ascription lies not simply in the question of whether or not Moses himself wrote the material, and it is a pity that since modern scholarship has judged that Moses is extremely unlikely to have written Genesis 12–50 (and the rest of the Pentateuch) the ascription has received little further thought. For part of the significance of the ascription resides in the basic context it provides for understanding the text.

Although the historical questions about the origins of Israel's religion are both complex and disputed, there is a general consensus that so far as anything can be said about the origins of

Israel's religion it is likely that it began with Moses.
Essentially, therefore, scholars follow the lead given by the
Pentateuch itself, where the foundations of Israel's faith—
God's self-revelation as YHWH, the Exodus, the passover, Sinai
and the giving of Torah, Israel's sacrificial worship—are all
ascribed to God's dealings with Moses. Of course, scholars
vary considerably in their assessments of the likely antiquity
of all these elements, and so vary correspondingly in the
extent of divergence from the biblical narrative in their critical historical reconstruction. But the point that the biblical
narrative is followed, at least in outline, is clear (and although
some scholars recently have wanted to abandon the biblical
outline altogether—see, e.g., N.P. Lemche, *Ancient Israel*—it
is not clear that any alternative account poses fewer historical
difficulties).

The corollary of recognizing that Israel's religion began
with Moses is the recognition that the patriarchal material is
intrinsically *non-Israelite*. Of course, it is not seen as alien to
Israel's religion, but is seen as Israel's precursor, i.e. pre-
Israelite, with which Israel in some way stood in continuity. As
we shall see, the patriarchal stories are full of divergences
from normative Israelite religion, which implicitly witness to
their intrinsically non-Israelite status. And here too, modern
scholars, following the lead of Alt in his seminal essay, 'The
God of the Fathers', have been inclined to follow the lead of the
biblical text, at least in outline, and to recognize in the patriarchal material genuinely ancient material which antedates
Israel's Mosaic religion.

It is in the light of these points that the significance of the
ascription of Genesis 12–50 to Moses can be appreciated. For
what it means is that those stories, although intrinsically and
originally standing outside Israel's faith, have been told from a
perspective within Israel's faith. This means, first, that these
stories have in some way been appropriated by Israel as its
own, and, secondly, that by ascription to Moses, they are told
as part of the authoritative and normative account of Israel's
story. The modern recognition that the material was most
probably not written by Moses but by a variety of authors in a
variety of periods all subsequent to Moses in no way affects

this basic point that the context from which the patriarchal stories are now told is Israel's context, a context different from that which they originally had. The present position of the patriarchal stories in the Pentateuch makes them part of Israel's authorized story of itself.

All this entails that reading the patriarchal stories is not a simple or straightforward matter. For the text presents both what the stories now *are*, part of Israel's story, and what the stories once *were*, part of a non-Israelite story. Although the more important of these two for the writers was clearly what the stories now are, for that is how they were to function as significant and authoritative within Israel, it remains true that many indicators of what the stories once were have been left in the text and not deliberately removed from it, and this not unnaturally encourages the inquisitive reader to enquire further about this historical dimension of the text. Whether the reader today is genuinely in a position to get behind the presentation of the material as it now stands in the biblical text is a moot point, on which opinions widely differ. But the point is that the enquiry is in principle a valid one, and one in some ways invited by the text itself.

This general point does not just arise from the traditional ascription of the material to Moses, but is present within the text itself. The one explicit and unambiguous place in Genesis 12–50 where the writer obtrudes his own Israelite perspective is Gen. 34.7, where the writer comments on the indignation of the sons of Jacob after the rape of Dinah with the words that Shechem 'had wrought folly in Israel by lying with Jacob's daughter'. For here 'Israel' is clearly used in the sense of a national community, a sense which it could not have in the patriarchal period.

If this general perspective on the patriarchal stories is correct, it still needs qualification in certain ways. For, as we shall see, there is much in the patriarchal stories that is not told in Israel's terms but retains its own distinctiveness. Moreover, the degree to which the patriarchal stories are told in Israel's terms varies from story to story. Generally speaking, it is in the stories of Abraham that the language and concerns characteristic of Yahwism are most present. It is likely, therefore, that it was the story of Abraham that received most reflection and incorporated most retelling when Israel made the patriarchal stories its own. A fuller sense of the varying character of the patriarchal stories should emerge in the course of the following chapters.

To summarize, the question of how to read the patriarchal narratives is not straightforward, both because of the legitimate difference of interest that readers may have, and because of the inherent tension within the text caused by the telling of non-Israelite material from the perspective of Israel. However, this complexity may add to the interest of the study—as will, I hope, become clear as this book progresses.

2

AN INTRODUCTION TO THE TEXT OF GENESIS 12–50

WITHIN THE COMPASS OF ONE SHORT CHAPTER it is hardly possible both to introduce all the content of Genesis 12–50 and also to indicate all the different ways of reading the text that have been proposed. What follows, therefore, is a selective introduction which seeks to highlight some of the major points of which the student should be aware.

The Character and Role of God in Genesis 12–50

As the narrative of Genesis 12–50 now stands, there are five major characters: Abraham, Isaac, Jacob, Joseph—and God. The most important of these is God, and it is he who provides the unity within Genesis 12–50 as a whole; as the human figures die and pass on, it is the consistent hidden presence and purpose of God who is preparing for his people Israel that runs through the material (compare e.g. Gen. 12.1-3 with 50.24).

The character of God is never described, but the fundamental assumption that is made is that this God is Israel's God, YHWH, and so some facets of his character can be presupposed in the light of what is said about YHWH elsewhere, especially in the four passages about the name, i.e. character, of YHWH in the book of Exodus (Exod. 3.13-15; 33.19; 34.5-7; 34.14). However, the fact that, according to the explicit statement of Exod. 6.3, God was not known as YHWH to the patriarchs suggests that at least sometimes in Genesis there may be

important differences in his character from his self-revelation
in Exodus.

For the most part YHWH is a presence who speaks and who
can be spoken to, but who does not usually appear in a form
accessible to sight and touch. However, he does sometimes
appear in the form (apparently) of a normal human being,
most famously to Abraham at Mamre (Gen. 18.1-33) and to
Jacob at the ford of Jabbok (Gen. 32.22-32), and is sometimes
represented by an 'angel' (*mal'ak*, literally messenger) who is
virtually indistinguishable from YHWH himself (Gen. 22.11).
Apart from his sometimes speaking and being spoken to in
apparently everyday circumstances (Gen. 13.14-17; 16.7-14;
17.1), there is a marked tendency for God to appear and speak
in visions and dreams (Gen. 15.1, 12; 20.3; 28.10-17; 31.24;
46.2). Sometimes the dreams are more pictorial and indirect
in their message—that is, they need interpretation, as is consistently the case in the story of Joseph (e.g. Gen. 37.5-11; 40.8;
41.1-45, esp. vv. 25, 32).

It is YHWH who provides the major continuity between the
stories, as everything that happens is to be seen as part of his
clear purpose, which is set out at the beginning of the patriarchal stories (12.1-3). This purpose, which will make of
Abraham a 'great nation', not only links the patriarchal
stories to one another but also links them to the story of Israel
which follows in Exodus, so that the Israelite who reads (or
hears) the stories will know that they are all part of Israel's
story.

Genesis draws attention to the meaning of the names of all
its principal human characters (Abraham, 17.5; Isaac, 17.17,
19; Jacob, 25.26; the twelve sons of Jacob, 29.31–30.24; 35.16-
18; the two sons of Joseph, 41.51-52; the fact that it never does
so with the names of any of the women, most notably the
absence of any comment on the naming of Dinah, 30.21, is one
small but significant aspect of the 'patriarchal' outlook of the
text). One might therefore expect Genesis to do the same with
the name of God. This does not happen, probably because the
meaning of YHWH is given in Exodus to Moses to whom the
name is revealed, and also because the Pentateuch retains the
tradition (Exod. 6.3) that the name YHWH was not known to

the patriarchs (despite the freedom with which it is used in the stories as they now stand). It remains interesting, however, to see how often terms other than YHWH are used for God— terms which once might have functioned as names, though not any longer as Israel's God has only one name, YHWH, and therefore other such terms are now to be understood as titles and epithets.

The most common alternative to YHWH is simply the generic term 'God' (*lōhîm). This is the main way of referring to God in the Jacob and Joseph stories. One significant feature of this usage is that it lacks the exclusivity implied by the name YHWH (who is specifically the God of Israel), and so is appropriate to those stories where there is a general openness about people's relationship with God. Thus when God speaks to Abimelech, king of Gerar (ch. 20) or to Pharaoh, king of Egypt (ch. 41), in much the same way as he speaks to Abraham or to Joseph, then it is the general, non-exclusive term *lōhîm that is consistently used. As we shall see later, there is a consistent openness about the depiction of God in Genesis 12–50, which forms a notable contrast to Exodus 3 onwards.

The title for God to which attention is drawn in Exod. 6.3 as characterizing God's self-revelation to the patriarchs is *El Shaddai*. The precise significance of this name is unclear, but it usually appears in contexts of a promise of future descendants (Gen. 17.1; 35.11; 48.3; 49.25). Traditionally it has been taken as a term expressing God's sovereignty—hence its traditional rendering as 'God Almighty'. Modern etymological study has suggested that its original meaning may have been 'God of the Mountain' (see, e.g., the discussion in Westermann, *Genesis 12–36*, pp. 257-58), but, even if this is correct, it is likely to have been unknown to the writers of Genesis for whom something like the traditional rendering is probably to be understood.

The Abraham Cycle: Genesis 11.27–25.18

The first of the patriarchs is Abraham (for convenience I shall consistently use the familiar longer form of his name, even though in terms of the story he does not acquire the name until Gen. 17.5). As already noted, it is in his stories that the divine name YHWH is most used, and so it is here that we most naturally look for the figure who was of most importance to the writers as preparing for, and in some ways prefiguring, Israel's faith.

Although Abraham is an individual figure, he is also often a representative or embodiment of Israel as a people. The opening words of YHWH to Abraham (12.2) draw attention to the fact that he is to be a great nation, and in 18.19 he is to teach his descendants to obey YHWH 'so that YHWH may bring Abraham what he has promised him'. As this refers to Abraham in the future, in the context of his descendants, it is clear that here Abraham himself somehow represents the people of Israel. Moreover, as we shall see, Abraham's stories are sometimes embodiments of Israel's story, both the Exodus and Sinai traditions. Thus the Abraham stories often need to be read on different levels, both for what they say about Abraham in his own right, and for what they show about Abraham as a type of Israel.

All the stories featuring Abraham are brief, usually corresponding to the length of a biblical chapter. This is somewhat different from the Jacob stories—some of these also are short, but those concerning Jacob and Laban form a more extended sequence. This is again different from the Joseph story which is predominantly one extended narrative. It is generally thought that these differences relate to the origins and transmission of the material, the Abraham stories having originally been short oral units, while the Joseph story has a more novel-like character. In terms of present function, the Abraham stories can more easily be used for didactic purposes, each one usually having some distinct moral or point.

From the outset, Abraham is a man of faith. When God asks him to relinquish everything that has constituted his identity and security—homeland, people, and family (12.1)—Abraham quite simply obeys ('So Abram went, as YHWH had told him', 12.4a). The first two things he does in the land of Canaan are to build altars to YHWH, thus indicating his responsive reverence to God's leading (12.7-8); the second time he builds an altar, it is also said that he 'called on the name of YHWH', that is, he prayed (cf. e.g. Ps. 116.[2], 4, 13, 17).

The most famous individual story of Abraham is Genesis 22, in which he is called to sacrifice his hope for the future in the person of his long-awaited son (see Chapter 3). This is the last story in which there is dialogue between God and Abraham, and Jewish tradition has often fruitfully linked it with the first dialogue in 12.1-3. There is indeed a verbal link between the two passages, in that each of God's addresses (12.1; 22.2) contains the otherwise unparalleled form of an idiomatic phrase, *lek leka* ('Go', but in fact similar to the archaic English idiom 'get thee' as in Hamlet's words to Ophelia, 'Get thee to a nunnery'). In ch. 12 Abraham is asked to go and relinquish his past, in ch. 22 he is asked to go and relinquish his future. Each time he trusts God and obeys without reservation. It is not surprising that Abraham has been looked to as a father of faith by Jew, Christian and Muslim alike.

Probably the overarching concern of the Abraham cycle is God's promise to Abraham of a land and a son (12.1-3), a promise whose fulfilment is delayed, so that Abraham has to live in hopeful faith. The promise of the land is to be fulfilled only in Abraham's descendants (12.7), so the crucial promise for Abraham himself is that of a son, since without a son there will be no descendants. For years Abraham has to wait. He jeopardizes the promise when he is willing to pass off Sarah into Pharaoh's harem (12.10-20); the promise is, however, renewed more than once (13.16; 15.5); yet although he trusts God in his promise (15.6), the actual fulfilment comes apparently no closer. Sarah's action of giving Hagar to Abraham may reasonably be read as showing impatience with the lack of fulfilment of the promise (16.1-6). When the news finally comes that a son is soon to be born to Sarah, this seems incredible (laughable) to both Abraham and Sarah (17.15-21; 18.9-15). The promise is jeopardized again when Sarah, presumably already pregnant, is passed off into Abimelech's harem (20.1-18). At last, Isaac is born (21.1-7). Yet even now nothing can be taken for granted, for it is now that God tells Abraham to sacrifice his son, and it is only when Abraham has

passed the supreme test of faith (22.1-19) that Isaac's future is
secure.

Other specific examples of Abraham's piety are not hard to
find. In ch. 13 he is prepared to allow Lot the first choice of
land (and it is ironic that when Lot chooses what looks to be
the most fertile part of the land, the southern Jordan Valley
['towards Zoar', 13.10; 19.15-22], the reader knows that this is
about to become the most notoriously barren part of the whole
land). In ch. 14 Abraham rescues Lot, is blessed by Melchizedek,
and declines any profit from his booty. In chs. 15 and 17 he
receives a covenant from God. In ch. 18 he not only shows
hospitality to strangers but is singled out as chosen by God for
moral purposes (18.19) and has the stature to engage with
God on the question of righteousness, probing the justice and
mercy of God (18.22-33). In ch. 20 he is seen as a man of
intercessory prayer (20.7). In ch. 21 he is recognized as someone of whom it can be said, 'God is with you in all that you do'
(21.22). And finally the fact that Abraham dies 'in a good old
age' (25.8) is a sign of the divine blessing which he enjoyed in
his life.

Particularly important is the fact that Abraham is the
recipient of a covenant with God in chs. 15 and 17. The word
'covenant' (Heb. $b^e r\hat{\imath}t$) is a term of central theological significance in the Old Testament generally, as this is how Israel's
relationship with God at Sinai is understood (Exod. 19.5, etc.).
Three points about this covenant may be noted here. First,
unlike the covenant at Sinai, where great emphasis is laid
upon Israel's responsibilities within the covenant and there
are severe warnings of judgment for disobedience (see esp.
Deut. 28), the covenant with Abraham lays its emphasis upon
what God promises to do for Abraham, to give him both descendants and land In this it is similar to the other three
covenants in the Old Testament that are made with individuals, Noah (Gen. 9.8-17), David (2 Sam. 7; 23.5; Ps. 89) and
Phinehas (Num. 25.10-13), all of which are essentially
promises of God; indeed it is notable in Ps. 89.3 [Heb. 4] that 'I
have made a covenant' is in poetic parallelism with 'I have
sworn'. It is not that there is no note at all about what
Abraham is to do (Gen. 17.1b); nonetheless the nature of the

covenant is clearly different from that at Sinai. The similarities between the covenants with Abraham and David have sometimes been considered evidence for the dating of the patriarchal material in the period of the united monarchy.

Secondly, it is a notable emphasis elsewhere, particularly in Deuteronomy, that God's election and deliverance of Israel are in fulfilment of the oath sworn to the fathers (esp. Deut. 7.6-8). Although this could refer to all the promises to the patriarchs, it is presumably particularly to the formal promissory covenant with Abraham that the reference should be understood. It is deeply characteristic of Israel that, although it sees its own faith as beginning with Moses, it roots its understanding of God's dealings in the pre-Mosaic patriarchal period and sees a strong continuity between the two.

Thirdly, it is initially perhaps a little surprising that the making of the covenant with Abraham is contained in two separate chapters. This is generally explained by the supposition that these were originally two separate accounts belonging to different sources (ch. 15, J and/or E; ch. 17, P—see Chapter 4 below), and this may well be so; certainly their styles are different, as ch. 15 has a vivid mixture of narrative and speech in a scene that is imaginatively memorable, while ch. 17 is almost entirely speech in a scene that has little development. Nonetheless, as the text stands there is a complementarity between the two. Gen. 15.7-21, with its mysterious ritual, focuses on the promise of land (15.7-8, 18), while ch. 17 focuses on the promise of descendants (vv. 2, 4) and on the need for circumcision as a sign of this. Presumably a major point of circumcision is that in the very act of sexual intercourse there should be an intimate reminder to both male and female within Israel that the child which is begotten is not simply the result of human processes but is also a gift from God in fulfilment of his promise.

Although piety is a major feature of Abraham's life, his piety is not incompatible with elements which are not generally considered pious. Abraham's first recorded words to God are words of questioning (15.2), and his response to the first promise of a son specifically through Sarah is incredulous laughter (17.16-17). Indeed, it is remarkable that in the very

chapter in which Abraham's faith is singled out for mention
(15.6) and in the one in which he first receives the covenant,
he responds to the two divine promises—which one would
suppose should simply be accepted with gratitude—with
questions about how he is to trust the promises (15.2, 8). This is
in fact a phenomenon akin to the laments in the Psalter, in
which the life of faith is envisaged as containing space for
questioning God without undermining the integrity of faith.

More questionable are two occasions when Abraham acts in
fear, jeopardizes the divine promise and brings misfortune
upon his host (12.10-20; 20.1-18), and also when he weakly
allows Sarah to deal harshly with Hagar (16.6; cf. 21.10-11).
The point is that even with someone as exemplary as
Abraham, the biblical writer is concerned to show the reality
of life with 'warts and all' lest an artifical kind of piety should
convey an atmosphere of unreality. As T.W. Mann has put it,

> Because the biblical authors persistently refuse to moralize,
> their characters are adamantly earthy creatures. Far from
> being cardboard stereotypes of moral virtue—or vice—they
> are 'credible' men and women of great and ultimately
> impenetrable complexity (*Book of the Torah*, p. 8).

Yet if there is a sense of moral ambiguity about Abraham, it
must readily be admitted that it is as nothing compared to that
which surrounds the figure of Jacob.

Isaac

The figure of Isaac is the least developed of all the major patriarchs. Indeed, it seems a little surprising that the traditional
patriarchal trio is Abraham, Isaac and Jacob, when the patriarchal stories actually concentrate on Abraham, Jacob and
Joseph. Nonetheless, the text treats Joseph differently, for it is
only to Abraham, Isaac and Jacob that God appears and
delivers his promise (12.1-3, etc.; 26.2-5; 28.13-15)—God is
never shown as speaking directly to Joseph. Thus Isaac does in
some basic way stand on a level with Abraham and Jacob, as
distinct from the twelve sons of Jacob.

One common attempt to explain the brevity of the Isaac
material has involved appealing to its probable history of

transmission at an early, oral stage. It is said to be a well-attested principle in oral and legendary material that a character who is originally of great prominence should recede into the background and have his position of prominence taken over by another character who becomes important at a later stage. In the light of this, it has been suggested that originally Isaac was a more prominent figure than Abraham. As Noth puts it,

> It is striking, even on first glance, that in the final form of the tradition which has been preserved for us, Isaac seems to be completely overshadowed by Abraham... Now the fact that Isaac recedes into the background in contrast to Abraham, the figure that manifestly evolved later, speaks for Isaac's priority... In comparison to Isaac, therefore, Abraham is to be regarded as the more 'modern' figure who, at the expense of Isaac, obtained more and more space in the tradition (*History of Pentateuchal Traditions*, p. 103).

While this is not impossible, one wonders how one should differentiate a figure who originally was prominent and later became relatively insignificant from a figure who was relatively insignificant in the first place—and given our lack of evidence or clear controls, such an issue can never be resolved.

In any case, Isaac is the least active and significant of the patriarchs. Alter interestingly refers to him as

> manifestly the most passive of the patriarchs. We have already seen him as a bound victim for whose life a ram is substituted; later, as a father, he will prefer the son who can go out to the field and bring him back provender, and his one extended scene will be lying in bed, weak and blind, while others act on him (*Art of Biblical Narrative*, p. 53).

Most of the stories about Isaac are primarily stories about either Abraham or Jacob (chs. 22, 24 [Abraham], 25.19-34; 27.1–28.9 [Jacob]). Only in ch. 26 is there a sequence of stories in which Isaac is the sole patriarch to feature. Yet even here almost everything has a parallel with what is said of Abraham:

26.1	A famine, as in the time of Abraham (12.10).
26.2-5	Divine promises, as to Abraham (12.1-3; 22.15-18).
26.6-11	Isaac passes off his wife as his sister, as did Abraham (12.10-20; 20.1-18).

26.12-14   Isaac attains great wealth, as did Abraham
             (13.2, 6).
26.15-22   Disputes with Philistines over wells (cf. 21.25).
26.23-25   YHWH appears to Isaac, who builds an altar and
             calls on the name of YHWH (cf. 12.7-8).
26.26-31   Isaac enters into a covenant with Abimelech and
             the Philistines (cf. 21.25-32).
26.32-33   The naming of Beersheba (cf. 21.31).

The effect of these similarities is to give a deep sense of pattern
and continuity between Abraham and Isaac—'like father, like
son'. Although there are differences within the similarities,
and these are important (see Chapter 4 below for the wife as
sister episode), it is the sense of continuity that is predominant.
The writer wishes to show a pattern of piety and blessing con-
tinued between the generations, though the advent of Jacob in
particular means that Isaac's final scene (ch. 27) shows him
as a less august figure than Abraham in his old age.

The Jacob Cycle: Genesis 25.19–36.43

Jacob is the most complex and enigmatic of the patriarchs —a
cunning and unscrupulous deceiver, who yet becomes a man
of God. He is the one who becomes Israel and so is the eponymous ancestor of the nation. One might have expected that
someone of the character of Abraham would have this honour
of being the eponymous ancestor of a nation called to be holy to
YHWH (Exod. 19.5-6; Deut. 7.6). Yet the fact that it is self-
seeking Jacob and not faithful Abraham who gives his name
to his descendants speaks volumes for Israel's understanding
of the nature of human life under God, and in particular the
ambiguous and paradoxical relationship between the call of
God and the moral response of the people called.

Jacob not only becomes the eponymous ancestor of the
people Israel. In some way he actually typifies and embodies
Israel. This is made clear at two crucial moments early in his
story. First, when Rebekah is suffering in her pregnancy with
Esau and Jacob she receives a message from YHWH that not
just two babies but 'Two nations are in your womb' (25.23).
Secondly, at the climax of Isaac's blessing of Jacob, Isaac says,
'Let peoples serve you, and nations bow down to you' (27.29)—

something which happens to Israel the nation in the time of David and subsequently, but not to Jacob the individual. However much, therefore, the story of Jacob and Esau can and should be read and understood as a struggle between two individual people, it needs also to be understood as in some way typifying the larger issue of the struggling relationship between nations, especially between Israel and Edom, who were generally at odds with each other in Israel's history.

This point, however, should not be applied automatically, as though everything in the story of Jacob and Esau were a cipher for the history of Israel and Edom. For, most obviously, the magnificent forgiveness with which Esau receives Jacob on his return from Paddan-Aram (Gen. 33.4—which Jesus may have used as the model for the father of the prodigal son, Lk. 15.20) is in no way expected in the light of the known history of Edomite dealings with Israel. This shows that the portrayal of Jacob and Esau as individuals has a value in its own right.

As the story of Jacob stands, it revolves around two remarkable encounters with God. The first is when Jacob is fleeing from home after cheating Esau out of his father's blessing in the memorable story of the deception of Isaac (ch. 27). While asleep in the open, he has a dream in which he sees a ladder set between earth and heaven, with angels ascending and descending and with God at the top speaking to him. The content of the divine address, God's first words to Jacob, is striking; not a word of rebuke for the deception of Isaac and Esau; instead, a self-introduction and four promises—land, descendants, blessing by the families of the earth, divine company and protection. (This emphasis on promise with no corresponding moral demands is, as we shall see, one of the many ways in which patriarchal religion differs from Mosaic religion.) When he wakes, Jacob is awed by the place, sets up the stone he used as a pillow as a sacred pillar, renames the place Bethel, and makes a vow (although he does not address God directly).

One attempt to do justice to the theological dimensions of the text has been to focus upon Jacob's statement 'how awesome is this place!' which has been taken as a classic expression of holiness, the sense of a *mysterium tremendum et fascinans*

(see R. Otto, *The Idea of the Holy*—although in fact, signifi-
cantly [see Chapter 5], the Hebrew word for 'holy' [*qādôš*] is
not used). A different facet of the text's significance is Jacob's
association with Bethel. In Israelite history, Bethel became an
important sanctuary (Judg. 20.18, 26; 1 Sam. 10.3), and so was
chosen by Jeroboam as one of the two major shrines of the
northern kingdom (1 Kgs 12.29). The present narrative
explains how Bethel became such a holy place. What is per-
·haps surprising is the implicitly positive view of Bethel that
the text contains, which has often led to the bulk of the text
being ascribed to the Elohist (see Chapter 4) writing in the
ninth century BC in the context of the northern kingdom
where Bethel was venerated. For elsewhere in the Old
Testament, Bethel is usually viewed negatively, both by the
writer of 1 Kgs 12.25–13.34 and 2 Kgs 23.15, and by Amos
(3.14; 4.4; 5.5) and Hosea (10.15). Moreover, given the implicitly positive view of Jerusalem in Genesis 22 (see Chapter 3),
one might expect a less positive view of Bethel in Genesis 28.
Perhaps the explanation is quite simply that the writer was
anxious to preserve the distinctive character of the patriarchal period as impervious to the later religious conflicts of
Yahwism.

In any case, Jacob's dream at Bethel makes clear that God is
involved in the life of Jacob, and this is important as a context
for understanding the following narrative of Jacob's stay with
Laban where there is little obvious divine engagement with
the situation and where Jacob and Laban take it in turns to
deceive each other. While Jacob is with Laban he acquires his
two wives, Leah and Rachel, and also eleven of his twelve sons.

The birth of the sons is interesting for the remarkably
matter-of-fact way in which it is told. One might have
expected that the birth of the eponymous ancestors of the
tribes of Israel would be surrounded by uplifting themes, but
the opposite is the case. For example, there is a famous little
vignette (30.14-24) of Leah gaining the right to sleep with
Jacob through Rachel's bartering acquisition of mandrakes (a
traditional aphrodisiac) gathered by Leah's son, Reuben. This
leads to the birth of more offspring, not only for Leah but also,
at last, for Rachel too. Although the writer is at pains to show

how in all this petty feuding God was present and working his purposes out (30.17, 22), the mundane nature of the proceedings is not disguised. All this is consistent with the emphasis elsewhere in the Pentateuch that God's choice of the people of Israel was not because of special qualities inherent in Israel (esp. Deut. 7.7-8).

A decisive turning point for Jacob comes when he has to return home with his wives and children, for now he is afraid of what Esau is likely to do to him. When he is told that Esau is coming to meet him with four hundred men, this seems to confirm his worst fears. This leads to Jacob offering his first prayer to God (32.9-12), in which there is a note of genuine humility and supplication (although, characteristically, Jacob has already started making his own practical arrangements to deal with the problem). But after further arrangements we read, 'And Jacob was left alone; and a man wrestled with him until the breaking of the day' (32.24). Of all Old Testament stories, this is perhaps the hardest to comment on, largely because the deliberately allusive and mysterious nature of the text makes the story appeal powerfully to the imagination but leaves it not very amenable to rational, discursive explanation. Is Jacob's adversary a spirit of the night, a river spirit, Esau, a projection of his subconscious, or God? As the text stands, it is clearly none other than YHWH in human form (32.30). But the fact that the story is suggestive of these other interpretations—perhaps because in earlier versions they were an actual part of the story—makes it likely that in a sense they are all true, as they all belong to the immediate or wider context of the story. God confronts Jacob not only in human form, but as Esau, whom he fears, as a night spirit, belonging to the time when his fears are at their sharpest, as a river spirit because he is crossing a perilous boundary into the territory of Israel, and as the embodiment of the deepest hopes and fears of his own mind. The writer boldly incorporates these folkloristic motifs in order to try to convey something of the mysterious depth of the occasion.

In the struggle Jacob is both victor and vanquished; he comes out with a new name, Israel, representing a new character as one who embodies what was best in the old character—he has

striven with God and men, and prevailed (32.28)—and as one
who limps, and will never stand upright in his own strength
again.

Hereafter, although Jacob/Israel is still recognizably the
same person, a change has occurred. After his reconciliation
with Esau, Jacob builds an altar for the first time and calls it
'God is the God of Israel' (33.20). Abraham from the outset
built altars as a mark of his faith in God; now Jacob does so too.
Some time later Jacob makes his family purge themselves of
'foreign gods' (the sole example in the patriarchal narratives
of a concern for religious purity in a characteristically
Yahwistic sense) and he builds another altar at Bethel (35.7).
In later years Jacob still appears as a poor parent who shows
favouritism among his children (37.3-4) and does not react
well to adversity (37.34-35; 42.35–43.15), nonetheless he is a
venerable figure who blesses Pharaoh (47.7, 10) and all his
sons (Gen. 48–49). The character of Jacob presents a fasci-
nating study in the difference that God does, and does not,
make in a wilful and recalcitrant personality.

One final point that may be noted about the Jacob cycle is
that it has certain similarities to the early story of Moses.
These may be noted as follows (for a fuller list, including some
looser parallels, see R.S. Hendel, *The Epic of the Patriarch*,
pp. 137-65, esp. 140):

1. Both Jacob and Moses do something that is morally
ambiguous (deception of father [Gen. 27], killing of Egyptian
[Exod. 2.11-15]) and consequently have to flee.

2. Both have a meeting with God at a holy place, which pre-
pares them for what lies ahead (Bethel, Gen. 28.10-22; Horeb,
Exod. 3.1–4.17).

3. Both meet their wife-to-be at a well (Gen. 29.1-14; Exod.
2.15b-21).

4. Both are told by God to return to the place from which
they originally fled (Gen. 31.13; Exod. 4.18-20).

5. Both have mysterious and threatening night encounters
with God (Gen. 32.22-32; Exod. 4.24-26).

How should these similarities be explained? Hendel suggests
that they show a common underlying oral narrative tradition,
and this may well be so. A shared tradition of storytelling about

significant figures in Israel's beginnings could well portray different characters in similar ways. However, this may suggest that the process could be largely unintentional. As we shall see later, the pentateuchal writers have a predilection for patterning and typology. It may equally be the case that Moses, as the founder of Israel's faith, was deliberately patterned on Jacob, the eponymous ancestor of the nation (or vice versa) to create a study in the similarities and the differences in the way God deals with the great figures of Israel.

The Joseph Cycle: Genesis 37–50

The main narrative about Joseph is the lengthy, novel-like story in Genesis 37, 39–45. Thereafter the material becomes more episodic, and Westermann (*Genesis 37–50*, pp. 22-24) argued that some of the material in chs. 46–50 originally belonged to the Jacob cycle. As the text stands, however, Joseph is the predominant figure. Chapter 37 starts with Joseph as a young man, and ch. 50 ends with his death.

Another distinctive characteristic of the Joseph material is the fact that unlike Abraham or Jacob there is never any hint in the text that Joseph typifies or embodies Israel as a people. Joseph is always and only an individual person, whose exemplary character is presumably intended to be taken as a model for other individuals also.

Although we first encounter Joseph as a somewhat priggish teenager (ch. 37), his experience of suffering seems rapidly to mature him into a serene man of faith who patiently endures unjust imprisonment, ultimately being rewarded by promotion to viceroy of Egypt. Although the precise extent to which he should be seen as an exemplary character is a matter of debate, there can be no question but that some exemplary elements are present in the text.

One of the most influential modern interpretations of the Joseph story was von Rad's essay 'The Joseph Narrative and Ancient Wisdom'. This has given rise to considerable debate (for a brief survey and bibliography, see Emerton, 'Wisdom', pp. 221-27). Insofar as much of Proverbs (a) deals with behaviour at court (e.g. Prov. 22.29), which is where Joseph

flourishes (Gen. 41.37-45), (b) commends the fear (i.e. obedience) of YHWH (Prov. 1.7) which Joseph displays (Gen. 39.9;
42.18), (c) commends self-discipline (Prov. 14.29) such as
Joseph shows in adversity, and (d) also generally portrays the
prosperity of the righteous (e.g. Prov. 10.6), just as Joseph
finally prospers, there are certain obvious general affinities
between the Joseph story and that strand of wisdom literature
represented by Proverbs. Within the story, Pharaoh explicitly
refers to Joseph as wise (41.39; cf. 41.33). The key theological
statements of the whole Joseph story are Joseph's words to his
brothers, 'So it was not you who sent me here but God' (Gen.
45.8) and 'You meant evil against me, but God meant it for
good' (50.20). Such an understanding of God's providential
sovereignty is also spelled out in Prov. 19.21, 'Many are the
plans in the mind of a man, but it is YHWH's purpose that will
be established' (cf. Prov. 16.9; 20.24). Even though there are
facets of Joseph that do not so readily relate to the emphases of
Proverbs—for example his skill in the interpretation of
dreams and his mysterious dealings with his family—there
are still enough similarities between Joseph and the concerns
of Proverbs for the parallel to be illuminating in reading the
text.

The explicit references to God's providential sovereignty
(45.8; 50.20) are all-important since they provide the context
for understanding all else that happens, in particular the
dreams that are crucial in the early chapters. Elsewhere in
Genesis, dreams are the context for a divine epiphany or
oracle (e.g. 15.12-21; 28.12-17), but here they are always in
the form of a sequence in their own right; they do not feature
God as such (in this the dreams are akin to parables) but are
given by God as adumbrations of the future. Joseph's recounting of his dreams to his brothers may have been foolish (an
example of when he did not hold his tongue [cf. e.g. Prov.
18.7]), but the dreams are clearly to be seen as God-given
anticipations of the story to come. The same is true of the
dreams of the butler and baker when Joseph is with them in
prison: he has the God-given ability (40.8) to interpret them,
and they come to pass as he has said. Most obviously is this the
case with the dreams of Pharaoh which only Joseph is able to

intepret (ch. 41). These dreams have received less attention than they might in theological discussions of the Joseph story, yet they are striking in that they go beyond the point that God can bring good out of evil intentions (45.5; 50.20) and show God knowing the future before it happens. Particularly striking is the statement of 41.32: 'And the doubling of Pharaoh's dream means that the thing is fixed by God, and God will shortly bring it to pass'. This implies that although sometimes there may be indeterminacy about the course of the future, this is not always the case. It is characteristic also of the practical nature of Hebrew faith that God's determination of a famine is seen not as an occasion for speculative questioning of the purposes of God, but for practical action on the part of the person (in this case, Joseph) who fears God.

Although Joseph is the central figure of these chapters, we are not given the insight into his character that might be expected. This has particularly puzzled readers of chs. 42–44 when Joseph does not reveal himself to his brothers but puts them through a series of hardships. What is his motive? Anger? Revenge? Testing? The text does not explicitly say. However, there are perhaps two clues. One is Joseph's tears when confronted by his brothers, which are the same for his brothers generally as they are for Benjamin in particular (42.23-24; 43.30; 45.1-3); this suggests that his heart is not set against them. The other is the explicit linkage between his harsh behaviour and his initial dreams (42.9); although the nature of the linkage is not spelt out, the fact that the reader knows that the dream is a God-given anticipation of the future suggests that Joseph's behaviour is somehow to be linked to the fulfilment of God's purposes. It is probable, therefore, that Joseph's behaviour towards his brothers, despite its puzzling nature, should be seen as some kind of well-intentioned test.

One final point about the Joseph story relates to its possible functions within Israel. One striking feature is its presentation of a Hebrew operating successfully in a foreign environment, and in this it appears to have been a model for the later books of Esther and Daniel (cf. W. Lee Humphreys, 'A Life-Style for Diaspora'). Certainly, when Jews found themselves in exile the story could have taken on an added significance as embodying some of the possibilities open to those who were willing to believe that YHWH could still be with them in exile. It may even be that the story received some editing in the exilic period. The otherwise slightly puzzling reference to Joseph's family being 'preserved as a remnant' (45.7) may perhaps make best sense if seen as a rewording of the story in the exilic period when this was precisely how the Jews in exile felt and when the story of Joseph was seen as offering some model for interpreting their situation.

Genesis 12–50 as Israelite Scripture

One final question to ask in this context is why Israel should have preserved the stories of the patriarchs. After all, Israel's own story begins with Moses and the Exodus, and it is only in this context that Israel's distinctive knowledge of God as YHWH is given. Although a partial answer may be that the writers of the Pentateuch wished to show a historical continuity between Israel and its antecedents, that of itself would not suffice to explain the position that Genesis 12–50 has at the outset of Israel's sacred writings, particularly when the religious ethos and practice of the patriarchs (see Chapter 5) is so at odds with that of Mosaic Yahwism.

I have suggested in *The Old Testament of the Old Testament* that Genesis 12–50 stands in relation to the rest of the Old Testament rather in the same way that the Old Testament stands in relation to the New Testament. Or, to put the same point the other way round, the familiar problem that the Christian has with the Old Testament is similar to the problem that Mosaic Yahwism and the writers of the Pentateuch had with the patriarchal traditions—in each case there is a conviction that it is the same God, but this recognition has to be combined with the recognition that somehow things then were different, a difference classically expressed in terms of old and new dispensations.

Although part of the reason why Christians have preserved the Old Testament as Christian Scripture is to show the historical continuity between Christian faith and its Hebrew and Jewish antecedents, this has not been the primary use to which the Old Testament has been put. Rather the Old Testament has been used as a resource for the life of faith, on the assumption that one can sit light to many of its specific religious *practices* (circumcision, sacrifice, food laws, etc.), and yet retain most of its religious *principles*. As long as there is a shared assumption that human life has value and dignity, that life is to be lived responsibly in trust and obedience under God, and that prayer is an essential medium of communication between God and humanity, then the religious principles that give rise to one set of religious practices in one context may still inform a distinct yet related set of religious practices in another context. It is likely that this kind of understanding accounts not only for Christian retention and use of the Old Testament as Christian Scripture, but also for Yahwistic retention and use of the patriarchal traditions in Genesis 12–50 as Hebrew Scripture. The primary interest of Israel in the patriarchs was therefore in them as people who could in one way or other exemplify the dynamics of life under God and so would inform and instruct successive generations of Israelites. This was in no sense a moralistic kind of exemplification, as we have seen that the portrayal of Jacob most obviously (though the same applies to a lesser extent to Abraham) is anything but moralistic—but is still usable to exemplify how life under God should (and should not) be lived.

If this understanding of Genesis 12–50 is at all valid, it should also be related to the well-known debate about the origins of Scripture as a significant concept within Israelite faith. It is customarily maintained that early Israel had little sense of texts as normative for faith, and that only with the advent of Deuteronomy in the late seventh century did there begin a movement in this direction. Certainly there is much in this notion, and one can easily see in Deuteronomy a concern for normativity that is lacking in other law codes (e.g. Deut. 1.5; 4.1-8; 12.32 [Heb. 13.1]; 31.9-13), and no doubt this did give considerable impetus towards Judaism's becoming increasingly centred upon a book rather than upon sacrifice in the temple. Nonetheless, if my proposed understanding of Genesis 12–50 is at all on the right lines, it suggests a concern for a narrative text such as Genesis 12–50 as also authoritative for Israel's faith. To be sure, it functions as authoritative in a way quite different from Deuteronomy, for Genesis 12–50 is a non-directive text, which much more obviously needs interpretation if it is to function as religiously authoritative than is the case with the legal precepts of Torah. Moreover, we do not know the date when Genesis 12–50 was recognized as authoritative for Israel, and whether this was earlier or later than Deuteronomy. Nonetheless, the point remains that any discussion about the origins and development of scriptural authority in Israel's faith needs to do justice not only to the laws of Deuteronomy but also to the narratives of Genesis 12–50.

3

A SPECIMEN TEXT: GENESIS 22

I PROPOSE IN THIS CHAPTER FURTHER TO INTRODUCE the patriarchal stories in general by focusing on one story in particular, Genesis 22. The hope is that the kinds of issues that are seen to be relevant to understanding this chapter will then be able to be applied elsewhere without too much difficulty. There is of course the danger that Genesis 22 may not be wholly typical of the patriarchal narratives. Indeed, it is in many ways distinctive in the range and depth of its content and in its mode of telling, and it is probable that the story has received more attention than others already in the time of the biblical writers, as well as subsequently. Nonetheless it is in my judgment sufficiently typical that it may serve to illustrate more clearly than most the kind of material that is found in a number of the patriarchal stories; it also shows the kinds of processes that we should suppose, to greater or lesser extent, to have been involved in the patriarchal narratives in general.

An Interpretation of Genesis 22

1. The first task is to read and interpret the story as it now stands. The best way to do this is to follow the lead of the story-teller. This, however, may be easier said than done, because, according to a famous analysis of the story by E. Auerbach in his *Mimesis*, Genesis 22 is a model of restraint on the part of the storyteller. The story is told in a taut, suspense-filled way, in which much is left unspecified by the narrator: 'time and

place are undefined...; thoughts and feelings remain unex-
pressed, are only suggested by the silence and the fragmen-
tary speeches; the whole...remains mysterious and "fraught
with background"' (*Mime*sis, pp. 11-12). There is much of
value in Auerbach's analysis; however, he has somewhat
overstated his case, for the writer does in fact provide strong
clues about the way in which the story should be understood.

Generally speaking, Old Testament storytellers do not stand
outside a story and comment upon it, but rather so tell it that it
conveys its own meaning. The points at which the storyteller
usually places what he considers most important are usually
the speeches made by the main characters at the dramatically
crucial moments, though sometimes repetitions and word-
plays also serve this function. In this, Genesis 22 is no exception.

Genesis 22 is, however, exceptional in that the narrator does
comment on the story and provides an explicit interpretative
key right at the outset, presumably because the story is not
only of prime importance but also because it may be liable to
misinterpretation. Thus the story begins, 'After these things
God tested (*nissâ*) Abraham'. The precise sense of 'test' will be
crucial to understanding the story, but it should not be taken
on its own, for there is one other word that should be taken in
conjunction with it. The speech of the angel of YHWH at the
critical moment of sacrifice refers to the result of the test, a
result which presumably constituted its purpose in the first
place, and so is essential to understanding it. Verse 12 reads,
'Do not lay your hand on the boy, and do not do anything to
him, for now I know that you fear God (lit. you are a fearer of
God, $y^e r\bar{e}$' $^e l\bar{o}h\hat{i}m$ '$att\hat{a}$), since you have not withheld your son,
your only son from me'. Here the crucial thing is that
Abraham fears God. Thus the two words which together provide the primary key to understanding the story are 'test'
(*nissâ*) and 'fear' (*yārē*').

The meaning of these words is best discovered by examining
their usage elsewhere. First, it should be noted that 'fear' in
Gen. 22.12 has its predominant Old Testament usage in a
religious context; that is, it does not indicate fright, or even
religious awe, but rather moral obedience. 'Fear' of God concerns doing rather than feeling (see e.g. Deut. 5.29, where

fearing God is connected with keeping his commandments, or Job 28.28, where the fear of the Lord is parallel to departing from evil).

Secondly, the words *nissâ* and *yārē'* occur together in one other passage in the Old Testament, that is Exod. 20.20, a key passage because in it Moses explains the purpose of God giving the Ten Commandments, the heart of Torah (the Hebrew word traditionally, but often misleadingly, rendered as 'Law'), to Israel. Here Moses says to Israel, 'Do not fear (i.e. be frightened), for God has come to test (*nassot*, the infinitive of *nissâ*) you, and so that the fear of him (i.e. obedience; *yir'ātô*, the noun from *yārē'*) may be before you to keep you from sin'. The purpose of Torah is thus in some way to challenge and draw out Israel into a fuller obedience to God. It should be noted, moreover, that although the specific words 'test' and 'fear' are not found in conjunction elsewhere, the concept that they represent is. For it is a recurrent notion, especially in the major theological treatment of Israel's position as the people of God—Deuteronomy, and literature related to Deuteronomy— that YHWH tests Israel so as to enhance their obedience to him; thus Exod. 16.4 interprets the giving of the manna in the wilderness as a matter of testing (*nissâ*) Israel, whether they will be obedient to Torah or not; Deut. 8.2 interprets the whole forty years in the wilderness as a time of God's testing (*nissâ*) whether Israel would be obedient to God's commandments; Deut. 13.3 [Heb. 4] interprets a wonder-working prophet who preaches apostasy as YHWH's testing (*nissâ*) Israel to prove whether they love him wholly and solely (cf. Deut. 33.8-9; Judg. 2.22; 3.4).

How then is the connection between Genesis 22 and these other passages to be understood? The linkage between the passages is routinely noted by most Genesis commentators, but most make little of it. Even Westermann (*Genesis 12–36*, p. 356), who has an excursus on *nissâ*, merely makes some observations about the history of the concept and points out that the usage of 'test' with regard to Israel as a people appears to be older than with regard to an individual person (such as Abraham). Yet the interpretation of Genesis 22 can be taken further than this.

Initially, it should be noted that the notion of God testing is primarily a part of a theology of Israel and Torah, for this is where the language overwhelmingly occurs, particularly in the key passage Exod. 20.20. It follows from this that the use of this language with regard to Abraham is an extension or reapplication. Why should this be? This is another instance where a basic perspective on the patriarchal stories as non-Israelite material told from Israel's context is illuminating. This may perhaps best be appreciated if we stand back initially and consider a well-known Christian analogy.

The Old Testament, as Christian Scripture, poses a well-known hermeneutical problem. If Jesus Christ is the supreme revelation of God, how is the Christian to understand and appropriate material from a pre-Christ context? One characteristic Christian assumption is that the Old Testament contains patterns and analogies to the revelation of God in Christ, a hermeneutical approach known as typology. Thus the basic Christian stance with regard to the Old Testament is Christological, that is, it starts with Christ, and reads the Old Testament looking for patterns and analogies to him.

Less well-known is the fact that the Old Testament itself contains a closely similar hermeneutical problem. For Israel, the supreme revelation of God is Torah, given by God through Moses to Israel at Sinai. Yet Israel used as part of its Scripture these stories of Israel's ancestors, the patriarchs, who lived in a pre-Torah context. How, then, was Israel to understand and appropriate these stories? The natural assumption is that they would want to show patterns and analogies to Torah, and to do so particularly with Abraham as the supreme exemplar of the life of faith under God. It is therefore not surprising when there is one explicit statement to this effect within the text (Gen. 26.5), and another of similar import (18.19), and when post-biblical Jewish tradition, from the Book of Jubilees in the second century BC onwards, extensively develops the notion that the patriarchs obeyed Torah even before it had been given at Sinai. Yet in fact it is not Gen. 26.5 that provides the best textual foundation for this notion, but rather Gen. 22.1, 12, where Israel's language of testing with a view to Torah obedience is applied to Abraham. For this makes Abraham an exemplary type of Israel, one who demonstrates as a representative individual the kind of Torah obedience to God that should characterize Israel as a whole.

2. The second main interpretative issue to consider, which is the one with which people tend to begin, is the fact that God is asking Abraham to take the life of a child. In any modern context this would be considered morally repugnant, and anyone who claimed to have been told by God to kill a child would find no credence for such claims from any responsible person, believer or non-believer. There is a modern tendency, encouraged (in different ways) by people of the stature of Kant and Kierkegaard to suppose that this modern moral judgment must also apply to the story in its ancient context. Yet such an approach is a classic example of anachronism and demonstrates the importance of having an informed historical perspective when reading the Old Testament. Our first point, about the nature of testing, indicates that the story is to be seen as a positive moral example, and this is confirmed by further considerations.

The general attitude to children in the ancient world was almost the exact opposite of that generally found in the modern West. Where the modern world has a high estimate of the value of children, which easily lapses into sentimentality, the ancient world had a low estimate, which easily lapsed into cruelty (most obviously in the widespread practice of the exposure, i.e. abandonment in the open to death, of unwanted children). The adult, in particular the father, was considered the norm of life, and children, until they themselves reached adulthood, were considered as significant to the extent that they enhanced the worth of the father. Although the Old Testament generally encourages a humane attitude towards children (and towards orphans and widows, being those most vulnerable in society because left without domestic male protection), it does not generally question their subordinate importance in relation to the father, and this is particularly evident in some of the older strata. For example, on two occasions in Genesis (other than ch. 22), the story takes for granted that a father can make life and death decisions about his child (38.24, Judah with regard to his daughter-in-law, Tamar; 42.37, Reuben with regard to his two sons). The law of Deut. 21.18-21 envisages a father's making a life and death decision with regard to a rebellious son, and Exod. 21.7 envisages a man's selling his daughter as a slave. Jephthah sacrificed his daughter in fulfilment of a vow (Judg. 11.34-40). The assumption common to all these passages is that the role and worth of the child is relative to, and dependent upon, the father. The material is, in one important sense of the term, patriarchal in outlook.

In the light of these passages, it is clear that Genesis 22 is making a similar assumption—Abraham naturally has the right of life and death over Isaac. Indeed, throughout the story of Abraham, Isaac is always seen as significant in terms of Abraham, for the birth of Isaac means that Abraham will no longer be without an heir by Sarah, and that the promise to Abraham made by God will be fulfilled. At the beginning of Genesis 22 something is said about Isaac, not about Isaac in himself but about his significance for Abraham ('your son, your only son Isaac, whom you love', v. 2), and at the end of the story it is Abraham who is commended and promised further blessing because he has not withheld his only son from God (22.16-18). The significance of Isaac in Genesis 22, therefore, is not that of a unique human being whom it would be immoral to kill. Rather, as Abraham's son, he is Abraham's hope for the future. Isaac is Abraham's most precious possession, a possession all the more significant because promised by God and waited for over so many years. What Abraham's test of obedience consists in, therefore, is a willingness to surrender to God that which is most precious to him, that in which he could most legitimately have confidence and hope, precisely because it was promised and given by God in the first place.

One other possibly relevant factor in this context is the widespread belief in the ancient Near East, shared also by Israel, that the first of all new life belonged to God. The underlying assumption was that as God was the giver of life, so he had the right to receive back the first and best of what he had given. In this, YHWH expected no less than any other deity, for in the context of the passover (itself a story about YHWH's life-

and-death authority over the firstborn) we read, 'Consecrate
to me all the firstborn; whatever is the first to open the womb
among the people of Israel, both of man and of beast, is mine'
(Exod. 13.2). Moreover, in Exod. 22.29-30 (Heb. 28-29) there
are some old laws about such offerings: first, agricultural produce ('You shall not delay to offer from the fulness of your
harvest and from the outflow of your presses'); secondly,
children ('The firstborn of your sons you shall give to me' [the
normal verb 'to give', *nātan*, is used]); thirdly, livestock ('You
shall do likewise with your oxen and with your sheep');
fourthly, there is a note that seems to apply to both sons and
livestock ('Seven days he/it shall be with his/its mother; on the
eighth day you shall give him/it to me'). It is often suggested
that ancient Israel at one stage countenanced the sacrifice of
children to God, and that Genesis 22 is a protest against such
practice. But whatever the underlying historical developments
may have been, the natural way of reading the Genesis text as
it now stands is rather different.

First, the premise on which the story rests is certainly that
God has the right to ask for Abraham's son (his firstborn by
Sarah), but less on the ground that this is God's right to the
firstborn than on the more general ground that God has a
right to ask for whatever he has given to Abraham. It is worth
noting that there are many similarities between Genesis 22
and Job 1–2, both stories where God tests a godly person, and
where the test consists of relinquishment of that which is most
precious. The attitude towards God contained in the famous
words of Job is not without relevance for Genesis 22: 'YHWH
gave, and YHWH has taken away; blessed be the name of
YHWH' (Job 1.21). The point in Genesis 22, however, is that
God is prepared not to exact his right to take away, but will
accept obedience and the token sacrifice of a ram instead.

Secondly, despite some resonance with the issue of God's
right to the firstborn, it may be correct to see that particular
issue as already dealt with, as the text now stands. The ancient
law of Exod. 22.29-30, cited above, does not specify the form
that 'giving' the firstborn to God should take, and only requires
that it be done after eight days. There is one obvious resonance
with this requirement that a child be given to God after eight

days, and that is the practice of circumcision on the eighth day (Gen. 17.12). Although Genesis 17 applies the requirement to every male child and not just the firstborn, it remains natural to see the law of male circumcision as a generalization of the principle of Exod. 22.29-30. This means that the practice of circumcision is, among other things, to be understood as the giving of a child to God. In the case of Isaac, this has already been carried out prior to Genesis 22 (Gen. 21.4).

In short, therefore, whatever moral scruples the story of Genesis 22 may initially arouse in a modern context, in its own context any notion of immorality is out of place. It is a story about God's demand of Abraham to relinquish to God that which is most precious to him, as the essence of what true faith ('fearing God') involves. God is able to demand this not only because of his intrinsic right to that which is best, but also because Isaac's life was God's gift in the first place. It is only as Abraham is willing to obey this hard command that he discovers that he will not in fact lose by it, but instead will gain great blessing (22.16-18).

3. A third major issue concerns the location of the story, something to which the story itself draws attention, both by naming the territory as Moriah (v. 2), and by recounting a special name given by Abraham in token of what had happened there (v. 14), a name given special significance by a wordplay (vv. 8, 14; see below). Where is this place?

The name Moriah occurs elsewhere in the Old Testament only in 2 Chron. 3.1: 'Then Solomon began to build the house of YHWH in Jerusalem on Mount Moriah, where YHWH had appeared to David his father, at the place that David had appointed, on the threshing floor of Ornan the Jebusite'. Although, surprisingly, reference is made only to the story of David (2 Sam. 24 // 1 Chron. 21) and not to the story of Abraham, there can be little doubt that the Chronicler's Moriah is the same as that of Genesis 22, and that a comparison of the passages means that the Temple is built on the site of Abraham's offering of Isaac. It is generally thought, however, that the identification of Jerusalem as the site of Genesis 22 is a later interpretation of the text which is not intended in the

story's own Genesis context. Von Rad, for example, comments
that 2 Chron. 3.1

> refers without doubt to the mountain on which the Temple
> stood. But our narrator means a land of Moriah about which
> we know nothing at all...He [the narrator] gives no place
> name at all [in Gen. 22.14], but only a pun which at one time
> undoubtedly explained a place name. But the name of the
> place has disappeared from the narrative...Perhaps the
> ancient name was lost because of the later combination of the
> narrative with the 'land of Moriah' (*Genesis*, pp. 240, 242,
> 243).

There are, however, good reasons for supposing that a reference to Jerusalem is indeed intended as an integral part of the
Genesis story as it now stands, and is the point of the pun in
v. 14.

There is an emphasis in the story upon 'seeing' (*rā'â*, 22.8,
13, 14; usually rendered 'provide' for reasons of sense in
context), which is related as a general principle to one place
where God supremely sees (22.14a) and is seen (22.14b). This
is probably to be connected with the name of the territory
where the story happens, Moriah (22.2), understood as a noun
from the verb *rā'â* with the sense 'Place of Seeing'. Within the
Old Testament generally, there are two places in particular
where God is seen: first, Sinai (esp. Exod. 24.9-11; cf. 1 Kgs 19.9-
18), and secondly Jerusalem (e.g. 2 Sam. 24.15-17; Isa. 6.1; Ps.
84, esp. vv. 5, 8 [Heb. 6, 9]). Since the story envisages a location
within the central territory of Israel, three days' journey from
Beersheba, it is naturally Jerusalem rather than Sinai that is
indicated.

Furthermore, the site of the story is linked with 'the mountain of YHWH' (*har yhwh*, 22.14b). Elsewhere in the Old
Testament the phrase 'the mountain of YHWH' is only ever
used of Jerusalem (Ps. 24.3; Isa. 2.3; Zech. 8.3), with the sole
exception of Num. 10.33 where it is used of Sinai.

Finally, with regard to location, one may note that the story
has to do with sacrifice, which for Israel, according to the prescriptions of the Old Testament, should supremely take place
within the Temple in Jerusalem. Abraham offers his sacrifice
to God at a place which God selects for him (22.2, 3), which is

similar to God's requirement for Israel's worship 'at the place
which YHWH will choose to put his name there' (Deut. 12.5,
etc.), a place which is to be understood as Jerusalem
(1 Kgs 14.21).

4. A fourth major element in the story, which has not yet been
considered, is the extended address by the angel of YHWH
when he calls a second time from heaven (22.15-18). This is
notable for at least two reasons. First, it renews God's promise
of blessing and does so in uniquely emphatic terms, stronger
than anywhere else in the Abraham story. Secondly, it links
this promise of blessing to Abraham's obedience ('because you
have done this... ; because you obeyed my voice', vv. 16, 18).

It is this second point that is theologically most interesting,
because elsewhere God's promises to Abraham are uncondi-
tional statements given with no grounding, thus implicitly
being grounded in the character and purposes of YHWH himself. I have studied this in detail elsewhere and have come to
the following conclusion:

> Abraham by his obedience has not qualified to be the recipient
> of blessing, because the promise of blessing had been given to
> him already. Rather, the existing promise is reaffirmed but
> its terms of reference are altered. A promise which previ-
> ously was grounded solely in the will and purpose of Yahweh
> is transformed so that it is now grounded *both* in the will of
> Yahweh *and* in the obedience of Abraham. It is not that the
> divine promise has become contingent upon Abraham's obedi-
> ence, but that Abraham's obedience has been incorporated
> into the divine promise. Henceforth Israel owes its existence
> not just to Yahweh but also to Abraham.
>   Theologically this constitutes a profound understanding of
> the value of human obedience— it can be taken up by God and
> become a motivating factor in his purposes towards man.
> Within the wider context of Hebrew theology I suggest that
> this is analogous to the assumptions underlying intercessory
> prayer... ('Earliest Commentary on the Akedah', pp. 320-21).

5. Although the main interest of Genesis 22 is in vv. 1-19, it
would be wrong to overlook vv. 20-24. At first sight the verses
are unpromising, just another of those Genesis genealogies
which seem to offer little to the modern reader. Yet it is not

accidental that the genealogy of the twelve sons of Nahor, Abraham's brother, has been placed directly after the preceding narrative, for in addition to the twelve sons, there is the intrusive mention of one woman, the granddaughter Rebekah (v. 23). The full significance of this woman within the Genesis story will not become clear until Abraham's servant goes in search of a wife for Isaac (Gen. 24), although the reader who, like the writer, stands within the context of Israel may already smile knowingly. What the narrator is doing is preparing the way for the fulfilment of the renewed promise of descendants to Abraham through Isaac (vv. 16-18) by quietly introducing, in a normal way, the human character whose life will soon be taken up into the fulfilment of the divine promise.

6. One final point may be made about the way in which the story is told. The restraint of the storyteller, which Auerbach interpreted in terms of suspense, may also be part of an imaginative desire to be faithful to the context of the patriarchs themselves which he is portraying. That is, although the writer is showing the linkage of Abraham with Torah and Jerusalem, he does not explicitly mention either, but rather leaves them implicit, to be inferred by the thoughtful reader from the clues provided in the text. Perhaps part of the reason for this is the recognition that in Abraham's own context neither Torah nor Jerusalem had the significance which they had for Israel. The writer's subtle, inferential reference to both makes it possible on the one hand to show Abraham's connections with what was central for Israel and on the other hand to respect his difference from Israel.

To sum up, what we have in Genesis 22 is a remarkable story of Abraham as a model of Israel's Torah-shaped obedience to God. He is willing to offer to God that which is dearest to him and he also offers sacrifice on the site of Israel's worship on the mountain of the Temple in Jerusalem. This obedience is understood to be of such value that it is incorporated by God into the heart of his purposes towards Israel.

From the point of view of a reader within the context of

Israel, it is also a story about how Israel's very existence hung, apparently, by a thread, for, had the sacrifice been carried out, there would have been no Israel. Yet the very fact that the story can be told presupposes that there is an Israel, and so from the outset the outcome is presupposed. Thus, together with the sense that God may himself imperil Israel's very existence, there is a sense that Israel will not fail, primarily because of the ultimate good purposes of the God who imperils, but also, and notably, because of the quality of human obedience that Israel's paradigmatic ancestor displayed. If the story is rightly understood, it is not only in God but also in an obedient human being that Israel's confidence for its existence is based.

A Critical Analysis

I have offered an interpretation of Genesis 22, and something of its riches and depths has been seen. Perhaps the best way to proceed further is by asking 'Is it true?' This question is the more important because of another feature of the way the story is told, as noted by Auerbach, and developed by M. Sternberg. As Auerbach puts it,

> Without believing in Abraham's sacrifice, it is impossible to put the narrative of it to the use for which it was written... The Bible's claim to truth...is tyrannical—it excludes all other claims...The Biblical narrative...seeks to overcome our reality: we are to fit our own life into its world... (*Mimesis*, pp. 14, 15).

Similarly, Sternberg refers to the

> Bible's determination to sanctify and compel literal belief in the past. It claims not just the status of history but, as Erich Auerbach rightly maintains, of *the* history—the one and only truth that, like God himself, brooks no rival...The Bible shows a supreme confidence in its facts. Any rival version, it implies, would be absurd, if at all conceivable (*Poetics of Biblical Narrative*, pp. 32, 126).

It is not important here to analyze the basis for such claims, for in one way or other some such understanding would be widely granted. The present concern is to explore precisely how credence might be given to some such claim about the truth of the text. This is not a question that can be answered without some careful exploration of precisely what is meant by truth in this context.

There is a recurrent tendency in much modern biblical study to approach the question of truth in a narrative via the question of its historical accuracy. For the great narratives of the Old Testament are certainly in some way historical narratives, telling the story of Israel from beginnings to exile. Moreover, from a theological point of view it has often been felt important to maintain at least a basic historicity of content in Israel's stories, lest the denial of such content would evacuate their value for the Christian believer who is committed to a belief in God's genuine engagement with life in this world. If, then, we approach Genesis 22 with the question of its historical accuracy in mind, what do we find? The short answer is—a problem.

The basic reason for this is the point I have emphasized as essential for understanding the patriarchal narratives, that they are pre-Israelite material told from an Israelite perspective. That is to say, by the very nature of the situation, the stories are told from a perspective that was not their own originally, and so far as this Israelite perspective has been incorporated into the text, so far has the original historical nature of the material faded into the background. If, for example, I am correct in the contention (see Chapter 4) that the Old Testament is consistent that the name YHWH was first revealed to Moses, and that all the uses in Genesis represent a Yahwistic retelling of the stories based on the conviction that YHWH the God of Israel is none other than the God of the patriarchs, then however much one may justify the procedure as theologically legitimate and in keeping with storytelling practice, the point remains that from a strictly historical perspective anachronism is involved—the patriarchs themselves in their historical context did not know God as YHWH.

To say all this does not mean that there may not be anything genuinely pre-Israelite still present in the patriarchal stories. As we will see in Chapter 5, there is considerable evidence that the Yahwistic tellers of the patriarchal stories were not only aware of the distinctively pre-Yahwistic, pre-Israelite nature of the stories, but also preserved this distinctiveness in many ways when one might have expected them to obliterate it. Nonetheless, the point remains that the writers did feel free to retell the patriarchal stories in their own terms and categories, and this makes the modern historical quest for the original form of the stories, not to mention their possible historicity, particularly elusive.

With regard to Genesis 22, this basic problem is obviously acute. The story as it now stands presupposes that Jerusalem is a holy site for Israel, and Jerusalem only first became Israelite under David in the early tenth century BC (2 Sam. 5.6-10; cf. Judg. 19.10-12). More specifically, it presupposes that the reader knows that the Temple stands in Jerusalem, which means that the story must be not earlier than the time of Solomon who built the Temple (1 Kgs 5–8). We do not know the date at which Israel developed its theology of testing and Torah, but it is most prominent in Deuteronomy and in Judges 2–3 which is written in the light of Deuteronomy, and these texts are conventionally dated to the seventh and sixth centuries; although Gen. 22.1, 12 and Exod. 20.20 may be earlier than these, it is obviously difficult to establish the point with much confidence. Finally, I have myself argued that the second address by the angel in Gen. 22.15-18 is an addition to a story that was already otherwise complete, an addition possibly made in the time of the exile in the mid-sixth century when the Abraham stories were probably being reappropriated as a foundation for Israel's future life after the exile (cf. Isa. 51.1-3).

For the content and composition of Genesis 22 as it now stands, we thus have to look to one or more periods within the general range of the tenth to sixth centuries BC. Yet on the timescale of the story itself, it is set sometime in the early second millennium BC—perhaps some 800 years before Solomon, and some 1200 years before the exile. If this timescale is to be taken at even approximately face value, then, for the historian, whose access to past events depends in the first instance on establishing the nature of the sources and establishing their likely degree of proximity to the events they relate, this means that strictly limited weight can be put on Genesis 22 as a historical source. For Genesis 22 simply stands at too great a remove from its narrated events.

The virtual impossibility of using Genesis 22 in its present form as a historical source may be illustrated by a consideration of one attempt to utilize it as such. For example, W. Harold Mare discusses the archaeology of Jerusalem in the Middle Bronze period (early second millennium). He notes Kathleen Kenyon's dating of a wall (above the Gihon spring on Mt Ophel) to c. 1800 BC, with its implications for population in the area at the time, and then comments: 'That Abraham did not encounter any opposition when he came to Mount Moriah to offer Isaac (Genesis 22) suggests that the inhabitants of the area were not strong enough or belligerent enough to organize resistance against him' (*Archaeology of the Jerusalem Area*, p. 24). The difficulty with such an inference from the text of Genesis 22 is that it seems to assume that had the local inhabitants been a significant problem, then they would have been mentioned (presumably as in Gen. 21.25-34; 26.17-22). Yet as Genesis 22 stands, such an issue is surely an irrelevance—the story is simply impervious to the question of what the inhabitants of the district might have been doing or thinking when Abraham was there. As far as the story goes, the only significant figures are Abraham, Isaac and God, and other people, outsiders, might as well not exist for all the difference they make. The assumption that Genesis 22 is just a simplified, selective account of historical events can, it is true, hardly be definitively refuted. But it is thoroughly implausible, partly because it does not take seriously the question of dating the source, partly because it does not take seriously the Yahwistic context from which originally non-Yahwistic material is now told, and partly because it does not sufficiently consider what type of material the story might be.

There are two main ways of trying to make progress in this apparent impasse. The first concerns the historian's desire to penetrate behind the present form of the narrative to try to recover something of its original pre-Yahwistic form. The

classic modern work in this regard was Gunkel's analysis of
the story in his *Genesis* commentary, which has been widely
adopted in subsequent works. Gunkel assumed that the story
told of the founding of a sanctuary (it being common practice
in ancient and mediaeval times for holy places to have official
stories of how they came to be), but that this must originally
have been somewhere other than Jerusalem. By assuming
that the uses of YHWH in v. 14 replace an original 'God' in the
form *'ēl* or *ᵉlōhîm*, and that the wordplay on 'see' (*yir'eh*, from
rā'â) is original to the story, he suggests that the original place
name given by Abraham in v. 14 was Jeruel, a place near
Tekoa mentioned in 2 Chron. 20.16, 20. Further, he assumes
that the sacrificial element was original to the story, and that
originally it told of actual child sacrifice to God at Jeruel,
though in time a ram came to be substituted for the child.

Such proposals are ingenious, but the obvious difficulty with
them is their speculative and untestable nature. Although one
may affirm the legitimacy in principle of seeking an earlier
form of the story, it seems arbitrary to retain the wordplay
and yet discount the links with the name Moriah and with
Jerusalem as the place of seeing, and also to retain the element
of sacrifice and yet discount the testing element altogether.
The main strength of Gunkel's suggestions lies in compara-
tive religio-historical study where stories about the founding
of holy places are not only common but are also liable to
retelling in the light of the concerns of those who happen to be
dominant at the holy place at any given time. But even this
really only reinforces the original insight, that the story has
been retold from a perspective different from that which it
originally had, and does not give any clue as to what the likely
original form may have been.

The alternative to penetrating behind the story is to focus on
the story as it stands, and in particular to ask what kind of
material the story is. The obvious category that comes to mind
is that of legend. This is a term that is often used so loosely and
diversely that it needs definition if its use is in any way to
clarify matters (see Auerbach, *Mimesis,* pp. 19-21; Hals,
'Legend'; von Rad, *Genesis*, pp. 31-43).

Broadly speaking, the main sense of legend is that of a story, usually attached to and originating from some outstanding and remarkable person or event, which is constantly told and retold and which in the retelling takes on a life of its own. This is a phenomenon attested in all cultures, and almost invariably the earliest history of a culture is cast in the form of legends (for example, the Homeric stories for the Greeks, the Arthurian stories for the British). Insofar as people have a sense of identity that is related to these stories, their retelling tends to embody the values and beliefs that are important to those who do the retelling. When the legend is of a religious nature, it often has a strongly moral element, aimed at encouraging imitation. This means that in due course the legend will usually come to say more about the beliefs and values of those who tell it and cherish it than it does about the person or event which originally gave rise to it—though obviously the relationship varies greatly from legend to legend.

It is in some such sense of the term 'legend' that Genesis 22 is probably to be understood. For it is clear first, that it is a story important to Israel's self-understanding and identity; secondly, that it is a story embodying a high degree of moral content of an exemplary nature; thirdly, that it was told and retold over a long period of time; fourthly, that in its present form it dates from a time when its content tells us primarily about the beliefs and values of those who told it.

There are at least two consequences that follow from this. First, we can only be agnostic about the bearing the story may have on 'the historical Abraham', for we simply do not have the necessary evidence either to affirm or to deny suggestions about the likely original date and content of the story.

Secondly, and more importantly, it should be clear that the question of the truth of the story is not primarily a question about the historicity of what it relates, but rather a question about the beliefs and values incorporated in the story by those who have related it. Presumably these beliefs and values arise out of Israel's life as a people under YHWH and have been incorporated in the story precisely because they have been found through practical experience of life under God to be true. Because the great figure of Abraham was the

outstanding exemplar of the potential of the life of faith under
God, it was felt to be appropriate to express Israel's understanding of basic truths about such life in the context of
retelling Abraham's story where such truths were already at
least implicitly present. In the legendary story of Abraham
there is a merging of past and present.

This means that the question about the truth, or otherwise,
of the story cannot be answered except by engaging with the
beliefs and values that the story portrays. Is it true to the character of God, and is it true to the nature of human life? These
are not questions that can be answered without reference to
one's basic stance as a person. In general terms, those who
stand in some kind of continuity with the ancient community
of faith which cherished and wrote the story and who themselves cherish it as part of scripture will be inclined to affirm
that the story is true. Those without that commitment may
answer differently.

4

WHEN, WHERE, BY WHOM AND HOW WAS GENESIS 12-50 WRITTEN?

THE SHORT, AND DISAPPOINTING, ANSWER to the questions of when, where, and by whom was the text of Genesis 12–50 written is that we do not know. The answer is the more disappointing because of the enormous expenditure of energy over the last 200 years or so into trying to determine the answer, and because, for most of the last century until the last 20 years or so, it was confidently thought by the consensus of biblical scholars that the answer was known, and was known in some detail.

The consensus may briefly be stated as follows. Some time during the reign of Solomon (c. 960–920 BC) an authoritative account of Israel's history, showing how God had led Israel to the highpoint of the United Monarchy was composed in Jerusalem by a writer known as the Yahwist ('J'—see below), who collated existing earlier traditions and transformed them into one consecutive account. This comprises the greater part of the narrative of the Pentateuch.

After the division of the kingdom following the death of Solomon, the northern kingdom of Israel produced a history of its own covering much the same ground as the Yahwist's history (which remained the official history of the southern kingdom centred on Jerusalem). The writer is known as the Elohist ('E'—see below), and the content and style of his history was influenced by the growing contemporary phenomenon of prophecy (especially Elijah and Elisha) in the

northern kingdom. After the fall of the northern kingdom in
721 to the Assyrians, this Elohistic history was preserved and
taken to Jerusalem, where it was combined with and merged
into the earlier work of the Yahwist to produce one new work
('JE').

In the seventh century, at about the time of Judah's breaking free from Assyrian suzerainty and of the initiation of
Josiah's reform (2 Kgs 22–23) the book of Deuteronomy was
written. Although Deuteronomy is a collection of laws and
exhortations distinct from the narratives of the Pentateuch,
the importance which it attaches to covenant as central to
understanding YHWH's relationship with Israel may have led
to some rewriting of the JE account of the Sinai covenant in
Exodus 19–24 and 32–34.

In the sixth century, at the end of the exile and during the
early years of the return from exile, there was another reform
movement, concerned that Israel should not repeat the sins
that had led to the exile. This movement was characterized by
the compilation of a large number of laws in such a way as to
regulate Israel's life as a holy nation. Because of the central
importance given to the priesthood and the correct perform-
ance of worship, this material is known as the Priestly
document ('P'). Although most of the material is presented in
the form of laws at Sinai, there is also a brief prefatory narrative covering the major points of Israel's traditional story, to
show how Israel's life as a worshipping nation was intended
by God from the outset.

In due course this most recent Priestly account of Israel's
history was combined with and merged into the earlier JE
account to produce one comprehensive account of Israel's
history. Although most of the narrative content of the history
was JE, the P material was used to provide the framework for
the whole.

This, in rough outline, is an account of the consensus view of
the Pentateuch. It was classically formulated by J. Wellhausen
in his *Die Komposition des Hexateuchs,* and his *Prolegomena
to the History of Ancient Israel.* It was mediated and rein-
forced in the English-speaking world by scholars such as
S.R. Driver, in his *Introduction to the Literature of the Old*

Testament, and in his *Genesis* commentary, each of which
went through many editions. It was modified by a variety of
scholars, especially von Rad, who, in his 'The Form-Critical
Problem of the Hexateuch' and his 'The Beginnings of
Historical Writing in Ancient Israel', won a consensus for
dating the Yahwist to the time of Solomon, at least a century
earlier than the date proposed by Wellhausen. In general
terms, there can be no doubt that it is a reconstruction of the
composition of the Pentateuch that makes perfectly good
sense.

So why is the situation so difficult today? The short answer is
that scholars have increasingly pressed the question 'But how
do you *know*?' For the fact is that the biblical writers made
themselves anonymous and invisible. They aimed to let the
text speak for itself, and nowhere in any of the texts of the
Pentateuch does the writer draw attention to himself or to his
context and his purposes in writing. Although by careful
analysis of the text it is indeed possible to discern differences of
vocabulary, style and emphasis and to make some suggestions
as to possible authorship in the light of these, the task is inevit-
ably a tentative and hypothetical undertaking. Although the
documentary hypothesis has commanded a scholarly consensus for many years, there has always been a minority of
scholars who have dissented from the consensus (often ultimately for religious motives, on the ground that the consensus
view impugned the integrity of the text, but still advancing
many cogent considerations). More recently, a growing
number of scholars, with no particular religious position to
defend, have questioned whether the scholarly consensus is
really as well founded as was supposed. The most cogent such
questioning is R.N. Whyhrny, *The Making of the Pentateuch*. \\

Admittedly the situation is far from being simply a return to
square one. Many scholars still maintain the documentary
hypothesis as the best available explanation of the text, and
even those who have abandoned it as a total explanation
usually retain elements of it (particularly relating to the
Priestly document). Nonetheless, the mood of the debate has
changed. It is academically respectable, in a way that it was
not previously, not to accept the documentary hypothesis

(although whether the respectability will endure will depend
on the strength of the proposals offered to replace it), and those
who do maintain the documentary hypothesis are conscious of
the need to justify and defend it afresh. Until recently it would
have been unthinkable for a reputable scholar to write, as does
D.M. Gunn, 'It is no exaggeration to say that the truly assured
results of historical critical scholarship concerning authorship, date and provenance would fill but a pamphlet' ('New
Directions', 66).

Even though the documentary hypothesis no longer holds
sway in the way it once did, it will never be possible to understand modern scholarly debate about Genesis 12–50 without
some knowledge of it, and so it will be appropriate to give further attention to certain aspects of the hypothesis, with special
reference to the basic arguments adduced in its favour.

The story of the development of the documentary hypothesis has often been told and is easily available; for short
accounts, see any Introduction to the Old Testament, and for a
fuller account, see R.J. Thompson, *Moses and the Law in a
Century of Criticism since Graf*. For present purposes it will
probably be most helpful to give a brief and highly selective
survey of the issues before moving on to examine one or two
specific examples to give a more detailed and first-hand
awareness of the problems.

The first clear setting of an agenda for a modern histori-
cally-oriented approach to the Bible was probably that of
Spinoza in the seventeenth century, for it was he who formulated the principle that, in study of the Old Testament, 'We
must consider who was the speaker, what was the occasion,
and to whom were the words addressed'. Instead of simply
considering what the text meant, and issues arising from that,
there was a new interest in when and where the text was
written, and in then interpreting the text in the light of that
knowledge. This was clearly a fundamental move in the
direction of 'reading the Bible like any other book' (as Jowett
later put it; cf. Chapter 1), specifically any other ancient historical text. As one recent Introduction puts it, 'The valid religious truth or "message" of the Hebrew Bible could only be

brought to light when seen as the religion of a particular people at a particular time and place as expressed in these particular writings' (Gottwald, *The Hebrew Bible*, p. 11).

Originally the assumption was made, following the tradition of both Jews and Christians, that Moses had written the pentateuchal text. Even on the assumption of Mosaic authorship, however, which would have meant that Exodus–Deuteronomy were contemporary with Moses, the book of Genesis posed particular problems; for what sources would Moses have had available to him, given that he lived some four hundred years (Gen. 15.13) after the patriarchs? Thus the composition of Genesis was the real issue in early pentateuchal criticism (and still today Genesis 12–50 poses problems different from those of the rest of the Pentateuch). Consequently, one of the earliest works of modern pentateuchal criticism was published in 1753 by Jean Astruc (physician to Louis XV) with the title *Conjectures sur les mémoires originaux dont il paroit que Moyse s'est servi pour composer le livre de la Genèse* ('Conjectures about the original documents which it would appear that Moses used to compose the book of Genesis').

One aspect of the text to which Astruc paid particular attention was the use of varying terms for God, in particular the regular alternation between 'Jehovah' (as he vocalized YHWH) and 'God' (*ᵉlōhîm*). In Jewish tradition this was an aspect of the text well-known since antiquity, and was usually interpreted solely in terms of difference of meaning, YHWH indicating God in his mercy, and *ᵉlōhîm* indicating God in his justice. As a total explanation of the alternations, however, this rapidly becomes forced and implausible (as do various more recent attempts always to explain the difference in terms of deliberate variation of meaning). Astruc's contribution was to reformulate the categories within which the phenomenon was interpreted, for he suggested that it was to be explained by two different source documents used by Moses, each of which had consistently used one particular term for God. Although Astruc's own analysis is not particularly cogent (for example, he simply divided Gen. 22 between his two sources—A, 22.1-10; B, 22.11-19—entirely on the basis of the use of *ᵉlōhîm* in

vv. 1-10 and YHWH in vv. 11-19 without regard for other considerations), the important thing was that he established categories which seemed plausible to the increasing historical awareness of scholars and which could be duly refined by others in the course of time.

Once the notion of sources distinguished by different terms for God became increasingly accepted, it was also not long before the assumption of Mosaic use of different sources was abandoned, mainly because of a growing awareness of different historical levels within the pentateuchal text. There was an awareness of the apparent anachronism of Gen. 12.6 and 13.7, which would seem to have been written at a time when the Canaanites were not (obviously or prominently, rather than at all) in the land, i.e. subsequent to Israel's entry into the land after the death of Moses. There was also a recognition of the great diversity of laws in Exodus–Deuteronomy, and of the fact that law is usually created and developed to meet everyday situations as they arise, and, consequently, that these laws seem to presuppose Israel's settled life within Canaan.

The factor that appeared to clinch the correctness of using different terms for God as an indication of sources was that of the passages which speak of the revelation of the name YHWH to Moses (Exod. 3 and 6). For the clear implication of Exod. 3.13-15 is that the name YHWH was only for the first time revealed to Moses, and the explicit statement of Exod. 6.2-3 is that this is indeed the case, and that God was known to the patriarchs not as YHWH but as El Shaddai. But how then is one to explain the fact that the name YHWH is used, and used extensively, in Genesis, where, according to Exodus 3 and 6, it ought to be unknown?

The scholarly consensus in modern times has been that the explanation is quite simple: there were two divergent accounts of the origin of the divine name. Where the name YHWH is used in Genesis, it is the work of a writer who thought that the name was then known; and so the writer is called 'The Yahwist'/'Jahwist' ('J'). It is supposed that Gen. 4.26b, 'At that time people began to call on the name of YHWH', is the Yahwist's account of how the name YHWH was known from primaeval times. Thus the Yahwist's history freely used the name YHWH throughout, and its existence as a distinct narrative strand is indicated precisely by the discrepancy with Exodus 3 and 6.

With regard to the use of *ᵉlōhîm* the situation is a little more complicated, as *two* sources characterized by this term were postulated. The first is that represented by Exodus 3, whose author believed that the divine name was first revealed to Moses. He is called the 'Elohist' ('E') because in Genesis, prior to the revelation in Exodus 3, he generally refers to God by the generic Hebrew word for God, *ᵉlōhîm*. The second is that of the writer of Exodus 6—considered to be a parallel account to Exodus 3 of an initial revelation of the divine name to Moses and not a sequel to it—who is known as the 'Priestly Writer' ('P'). In Genesis, P generally refers to God as *ᵉlōhîm*, but his most distinctive appellation is El Shaddai (traditionally rendered 'God Almighty'), as specified in Exod. 6.3 and used at the beginning of Genesis 17 (the priestly account of God's covenant with Abraham), Gen. 28.3 (the priestly account of Jacob's departure to Aram) and Gen. 35.11; 48.3 (the priestly account of God's appearance to Jacob at Bethel). (The other two uses of El Shaddai in Genesis, 43.14 and 49.25, are less significant, and opinion has been divided as to whether or not they belong to P.)

The documentary hypothesis has been developed with reference to a large number of other factors. But insofar as it relates to pentateuchal narratives, the above factor of the terms used for God has been central. Thus one can find M. Noth and A. Weiser, two distinguished proponents of the documentary hypothesis, saying, 'Regardless of scholarly ingenuity, no one has offered a more plausible explanation of the usage of the divine names than the view that these were two originally independent narrative works, the "Yahwist" and the "Elohist", which were later combined' (*A History of Pentateuchal Traditions*, p. 23), and 'Exod. 3 and 6 enables us to see that the use of different names for God is based on quite definite theories which point to different trends in the separate sources' (*Introduction to the Old Testament*, p. 74).

Despite the consensus it has commanded, this approach to the text does create a number of difficulties of its own (see my

The Old Testament of the Old Testament, ch. 2, for fuller discussion), of which perhaps the most serious is the question
whether the writers of the Pentateuch, if they had supposed
themselves to possess two fundamentally divergent accounts
of a matter so important as the origin of the name of Israel's
God, would have juxtaposed the discrepant sources in the way
the hypothesis requires without making some resolution of the
problem.

As already noted, the scholarly consensus around the documentary hypothesis has never been unanimous. A traditional
and modern conservative alternative, persistently held by a
minority of scholars, has been to argue that the name YHWH
was indeed known to the patriarchs prior to Moses, and that
the point of Exodus 3 and 6 is not the giving of a new name but
simply the giving of a new meaning and significance to an
already familiar name. Thus there is no discrepancy of traditions. This argument, however, faces two major obstacles. One
is the explicit statement of Exod. 6.3, 'I appeared to Abraham,
to Isaac, and to Jacob as El Shaddai, and by my name YHWH I
was not known to them', which has to be forced to have a
meaning other than the plain sense of the Hebrew. The other
is the simple fact that the meaning which the divine name has
in Genesis in no way differs from that which it has elsewhere.

This leaves us with one other possible resolution of the problem. This is to suppose that the Old Testament is indeed consistent in its contention that the name YHWH was first revealed
by God to Moses, and that all the uses of the name in Genesis
simply indicate the retelling of the patriarchal stories from the
context and perspective of Mosaic Yahwism. That is, the
Genesis narrators stand within Israel whose God is YHWH, but
they take for granted that Israel's God is one and the same as
the God of Israel's ancestors, the patriarchs, and so feel free to
use the familiar name for Israel's God when telling the patriarchal stories. Although from a strictly historical perspective
such usage involves anachronism, this kind of merging of perspectives is common practice among storytellers both in the
ancient world and subsequently. The issue at stake, therefore,
is not that of differing views as to the origin of the divine name,
maintained by different sources. Rather it is essentially a

theological issue, a combination of the particularist conviction that YHWH has only revealed his name and commandments within Israel, with the universal conviction that YHWH is the one true God and that he is therefore the God with whom Israel's ancestors had to do.

Why then the alternation between different terms for God? On my proposed view, the basic and original term for God in the patriarchal stories was *ᵉlōhîm*. As a generic title for God, without the particularity implied by YHWH, it is consistent with what we shall see to be the open and inclusive religious outlook of the patriarchal narratives generally (see Chapter 5). The name El Shaddai is a particular name, used on occasion in certain circumstances, whose precise significance is unclear, but which is generally connected with promises of blessing and descendants. El Shaddai is in fact one of a number of divine appellations compounded with El (e.g. El Elyon, Gen. 14.18, 19, 20, 22; El Elohe Israel, 33.20). As we know that the high God of the indigenous religion of Syria and Canaan in the second millennium BC was called El (see the Ugaritic texts from Ras Shamra in N. Syria, conveniently available either in J. Pritchard, *Ancient Near Eastern Texts Relating to the Old Testament* or D. Winton Thomas, *Documents from Old Testament Times*), it again fits well with the inherently non-Yahwistic character of patriarchal religion. The name YHWH is used in general because of the telling from a Yahwistic perspective, and so sometimes could be a term loosely interchangeable with *ᵉlōhîm* for no particular reason. It is, however, notable that the name YHWH is most used in the stories of Abraham, and it is precisely here that one finds the greatest other evidence for Yahwistic perspectives also. That is, it is apparent that it was the figure of Abraham that received most theological reflection and moulding from the Israelite narrators (as seen most clearly in Gen. 22), and that therefore the extensive use of YHWH in the stories of Abraham is part of a much wider theological appropriation of the material.

If this is at all on the right lines, it suggests that the basic model of different sources may not be as such incorrect but may still not be the best way of conceptualizing the issue. Rather, the model of retelling from a new perspective may be much more helpful. Take, for example, the Joseph story (Gen. 37–50). Although this is a narrative conventionally divided between J, E and P, it is notable that the divine name YHWH only occurs in three contexts. It appears in Gen. 49.18 in what looks to be a comment that has been added to the text. It appears in Gen. 38.7, 10 in two comments which draw an explicit moral lesson, in a story whose relationship to the surrounding Joseph story is in any case somewhat unclear. And it appears eight times in the narrator's interpretative comments at the beginning and end of the story of Joseph and Potiphar's wife in Genesis 39 (vv. 2, 3, 5, 21, 23), where it may naturally be seen as an explicit telling of this part of Joseph's story in terms of the purposes of YHWH, thereby setting the context for all else that happens to Joseph in Egypt. Surely the best explanation of this phenomenon is not that of a distinct source using YHWH, but rather of a narrator and/or editor retelling existing material and adding explicit reference to YHWH in the process. It would also be in keeping with what we saw to be the case in Genesis 22, where the story of Abraham and Isàac has been much retold and has incorporated perspectives from its retellings.

Nor is this kind of proposal unprecedented in recent debate, for the main alternative to the documentary hypothesis has been R. Rendtorff's proposals in his *The Problem of the Process of Transmission in the Pentateuch,* which have been further developed by his pupil E. Blum in his *Die Komposition der Vätergeschichte.* Rendtorff argues that instead of thinking of sources which run as continuous threads through the Pentateuch (the originally independent and parallel histories of J, E and P), we should think of distinct traditions which originally existed in their own right and then were subsequently brought together and edited to establish links between them. Rendtorff's own specific proposals for seeing the divine promises as such a link are in my judgment somewhat tenuous, but his basic model has much to commend it. If it is right to see the patriarchal narratives as a whole as a body of tradition appropriated and retold in a Yahwistic context, then similar processes may also have been at work within the individual patriarchal narratives, the stories of Abraham, Jacob and Joseph as originally told separately having been subsequently combined and retold.

A Test Case: The Patriarch in Danger through his Wife

Apart from the criterion of different terms for God as a clue to how the text of Genesis was written, the other criterion most appealed to in this context is that of 'doublets' in the text. M. Noth even puts this as the first of his criteria:

> Fundamentally only one of the usual criteria for the disunity of the old Pentateuchal tradition is really useful, though this one is quite adequate and allows a thoroughgoing literary analysis. I refer to the unquestionable fact, attested time and again throughout the tradition, of the *repeated occurrence* of the same narrative materials or narrative elements *in different versions*...The only possible explanation of the matter is that in the old Pentateuchal tradition several originally independent parallel strands of narrative were later connected with one another (*History of Pentateuchal Traditions*, pp. 21, 22).

One of the examples of this phenomenon most cited in this connection is the story of the endangering of the patriarch through his wife in Gen. 12.10-20 // 20.1-18 // 26.6-11, so it will be worth considering this in some detail.

A quick review of the three stories will show that they have a certain basic plot in common. Each time the patriarch travels south to alien territory and sojourns there; each time the patriarch fears death because of his wife; each time the patriarch resolves the problem by passing off his wife as his sister; each time the patriarch is found out by the foreign ruler, who upbraids him with the words 'What have you done to me/us?'. How should this be understood? As the text stands, these are clearly consecutive episodes which show a strong sense of pattern and repetition within the patriarchal story. However, just as the understanding of the phenomenon of different terms for God was seen by Astruc as evidence for different underlying sources, so too with the phenomenon of doublets. The usual assumption that has been made is that one writer would not have repeated himself in the manner of the present text, and so the different forms of the story must derive from different sources. Moreover, the similarities between the different accounts show that in fact there is really only one story with which we are dealing. There was one original story which was told in a variety of ways in a variety of contexts, the differences of detail between the present versions being essentially an accident of the retelling process. The different pentateuchal sources each knew of the same story in a different form, and when the sources were combined by a redactor they were then made into successive, rather than parallel, episodes—either because the differences of detail led the redactor to suppose that the stories were in fact distinct, or because to make them sequential was the only way in which the redactor could preserve all the versions of the story without having to lose any.

The question which story should be ascribed to which source is then reasonably straightforward, at least for Genesis 12 and 20. Gen. 12.10-20 is considered to be the work of the Yahwist, partly because the story uses the name YHWH (v. 17), and partly because the brevity with which the story is told, lacking elaboration or justification, is suggestive of its great antiquity. J. Skinner, for example, commented that the content of the story is 'treated with a frank realism which seems to take us down to the bed-rock of Hebrew folklore' (*Genesis*, pp. 247-48). Genesis 20, by contrast, is the work of the Elohist. The term *ᵉlōhîm* is used throughout (apart from v. 18, which looks like a later explanatory gloss); Abraham is said to be a prophet, thus revealing the links of the Elohist with the prophetic movement in the northern kingdom; and the story throughout shows a much more developed moral and religious awareness than is the case in Genesis 12 and so is not only later but also most probably linked to the moral concerns of the prophetic tradition (note such words as 'righteous' [v. 4], 'integrity' [vv. 5, 6], 'sin' [vv. 6, 9], 'fearing' [vv. 8, 11]). Gen. 26.6-11 is the most difficult story to place, since there is no term for God, nor do any distinctive vocabulary or concepts occur in it. However, the use of YHWH in the surrounding context (vv. 2, 12), together with the general narrative style, has inclined commentators to ascribe the story to J, although some have indicated their unease (it would require repetition within J, when one of the basic premises is that J would not have repeated things) by proposing that it may be a later version of, or addition to, J.

As to the original form that the story took, this can only be a matter of surmise. Although Genesis 12 is considered the oldest form of the stories as they now stand, it does not follow that it is necessarily the original. K. Koch compares the stories under eight headings and arrives at the following reconstruction:

> The original version will thus have run: Because of famine Isaac travelled from the desert in southern Palestine to the nearby Canaanite city of Gerar, to live there as 'sojourner', i.e. to keep within the pasturage rights on the ground belonging to the city. He told everyone that his wife was his sister so that his life would not be endangered by those who desired her. However, Rebekah's beauty could not pass unnoticed. The king of the city, Abimelech, took Rebekah into his harem, amply compensating Isaac. As a material sin was about to be committed, God struck the people of the palace with a mysterious illness. Through the medium of his gods, or a soothsayer, Abimelech recognised what had happened. Abimelech called Isaac to account: 'What is this that you have done to me?' He then restored him his wife and sent him away, loaded with gifts (*Growth of the Biblical Tradition*, p. 126).

What should one make of this? First, in general historical terms, there is clearly no difficulty in imagining the kind of process here proposed, which is both coherent and plausible as an account of how a story can develop and change. Secondly, one may always legitimately quibble at details of the proposed original version, which must necessarily be hypothetical. One major decision is that the story originally belonged to Isaac rather than Abraham, on the principle, noted above, that often in oral tradition figures change their importance, a principle whose application is necessarily controversial.

Thirdly, one should note some difficulty with the initial assumption that similar stories are really variants of one story from different sources on the grounds that one writer would not repeat himself in this way. For, of course, this is precisely what the hypothesis requires the redactor who put the sources together to have done. One might try to ease the problem by saying that in the original creative period of writing (J and E) such repetition would not have been permitted, but that by the time of the redactor there was less creativity and more sense of the need for reverential preservation of received tradition. Yet even this is of limited validity, partly because it seems an unfounded and romanticist notion to extol J and E as free and creative and to stigmatize the redactor as a pious collator, not least because there is little or no evidence that by the probable time of the redactor literary conventions had changed in any significant way, and partly because of the inconsistency that elsewhere the redactor is at times held to have exercised great freedom in his handling of the traditions before him.

Despite the fact that the proposed process is still not implausible, one should nonetheless ask whether it is a relevant consideration. It is important not to beg the question by assuming that one knows what kind of problem the text presents us with, when a decision here is in fact controversial. Is the interpretation of apparently puzzling factors in the text really best explained on the assumption of different sources? I have argued that this is probably not the case with differing terms for God, which should be understood rather in terms of storytelling technique, retelling old material in new categories. May this phenomenon of similar stories not also be explained similarly? On any reckoning, the fundamental question posed by the Old Testament text relates to the storytelling conventions of the ancient narrator. What conventions were taken for granted by the narrator? Obviously this can never be definitively answered, becaue all we have to go on is the text itself which offers no explanations. The goal of the scholar is a careful and sympathetic reading of the text that allows one to infer at least some of what the conventions embodied in the text may have been.

Why then should similar stories be told in proximity to each other in the course of the Genesis narrative? Instead of seeing this as a question of origins, it may be a question of creative storytelling. One way of putting this is to observe that whereas traditional source analysis emphasizes the similarities between the stories, seeing the differences as accidents of oral tradition, it may be the case that it is the differences that are really significant. Robert Alter has argued for the importance in ancient storytelling of 'type-scenes' in which a scenario familiar to both storyteller and audience is presented. Given the familiarity of the scenario, the interest lies each time in the particular way each story is told, or, in other words, in those elements of the story that are peculiar to it and which distinguish it from other versions. If this assumption is at all correct—and it too has obvious plausibility—then it is not a problem that a narrator should include similar stories in proximity to each other; rather it is to be expected. Indeed, we have already noted (Chapter 2) that Genesis 26 contains every story that is told of Isaac in his own right, and that each one is parallel to something that is told of Abraham. It is misleading to single out 26.5-11 as though it presented particular problems, when almost everything in the chapter presents the same issue. Thus the clear propensity of the text for repeating material in slightly different form surely directs us in the first instance to a phenomenon of ancient Hebrew storytelling, and is only secondarily, if at all, indicative of the possibly diverse sources and origins of the material.

If then we consider the three stories as type scenes, a number of factors emerge. First, apart from the similarities noted above, there are certain further similarities. On the one hand, on the first two appearances of the type-scene the incident represents a threat to God's promise. The scene first appears just after the promise has initially been given (Gen. 12.1-3). Its second occurrence is when the promise has been finally affirmed for Sarah herself (Gen. 18.14) and when in fact Sarah must already be pregnant with Isaac. Thus on both occurrences there is a sense of human fear and weakness endangering yet not thwarting the divine purpose. On the other hand, each story portrays the patriarch, the recipient of God's promise and the agent of God's future blessing, in a morally ambiguous light. When each time the deceived king asks 'What is this you have done to me/us?' it is difficult not to feel that his moral indignation is justified. The mysterious nature of God's call is thus explored, particularly in Genesis 20, where Abimelech's initial question to God, 'Lord, will you slay an innocent (literally, righteous, *ṣaddīq*) people?' is closely

similar to Abraham's own famous interaction with God (Gen.
18.23)—those whom God does not call may still have moral
insights similar to those of the ones who are called.

As for the differences between the stories, 12.10-20 should
probably be understood typologically, in a way analogous to
Genesis 22, where Abraham is a type of obedience to Torah.
For here an Exodus typology can easily be discerned. In time
of famine in Canaan, Abraham goes down to Egypt, as do the
sons of Jacob (cf. Gen. 42–46); there he prospers, as does Israel
(cf. Exod. 1.7); YHWH afflicts Pharaoh and his house with
great plagues, as he does at the time of the Exodus (cf.
Exod. 7–12); Abraham is subsequently sent out from Egypt,
and departs for Canaan as Israel does (cf. Exod. 12.31; 13.4-5);
and Abraham leaves with great wealth and possessions, as
does Israel (cf. Exod. 12.35, 38).

Genesis 20, by contrast, seems to explore the ambivalent
relationship between Abraham, representing Israel, and
Abimelech, representing upright (*ṣaddîq*) gentiles. As already
noted, Abimelech has a moral insight similar to that of
Abraham himself. Nonetheless, the election and responsibility
of Abraham is maintained, particularly in v. 7, which may
well be a picture of the relationship between Israel and the
nations: Israel has the privilege and responsibility of a special
relationship with God, and however much this is compro-
mised by doubtful behaviour, the importance of praying for
the life and wellbeing of others remains.

Gen. 26.6-11 is again different. First, although the episode
appears after a renewed divine promise of multiplying Isaac's
descendants, this time the promise is not imperilled, because
Jacob and Esau have already been born. This time the reader
may relax and smile—the stakes are lowered. Secondly,
Rebekah is never taken into a harem. All that happens is told
in a wordplay when Abimelech sees Isaac fondling (*yiṣḥāq
mᵉṣaḥēq*) Rebekah. Neither of the other stories say anything
about what happens to the wife, and now when something
does happen it is a bit of conjugal love-play.

Thus the first type-scene depicts Israel's triumph over Egypt,
the second depicts a more ambiguous and yet still defined
relationship between Israel and gentile neighbours, and the

third is a relaxed and humorous variation on the theme.

In conclusion, it may be said that the major problem facing discussions about the composition of Genesis 12–50 is a conceptual one. Within what categories should the data of the text be interpreted? Although the move, epitomized by Astruc, of interpreting data in terms of underlying sources has been profoundly influential, it is not in fact a good starting-point, because it begs the question. The first question that must be asked is about the storytelling conventions and techniques of the Genesis writers, and only when that has been established with as much confidence as is possible can one move on to ask about the evidence the text provides for the history of its composition. And although it may well be the case that different sources are combined in Genesis, I have suggested that the primary model for understanding the compositional processes should be that of the retelling and remoulding of old stories in the light of new perspectives. It is only as one focuses first on the 'how' of biblical storytelling that one may be able to answer questions about the 'when', 'where', and 'by whom'.

5

A HISTORICAL
PROBE

IN THE DISCUSSION THUS FAR THE ASSUMPTION has been made that the patriarchal narratives in general represent genuinely ancient, pre-Israelite, material which has been retold from the perspective of Mosaic Yahwism. This assumption is itself controversial, however, and it will therefore be appropriate to explore and justify it in this chapter.

One well known problem which can easily be accommodated on the model of later retelling is that of anachronisms. For example, it has often been argued that in the early second millennium the camel was not yet domesticated (it is an argument from silence, since the camel is not mentioned or depicted where it might be expected, but reasonably cogent nonetheless), and yet the patriarchs are depicted with camels (e.g. Gen. 12.16; 24.10-67). Again, the Philistines are reckoned not to have arrived in Palestine until the end of the second millennium, yet they are depicted as contemporary with Abraham and Isaac (Gen. 20.32; 26.14-18). Assuming, for the sake of argument, that it is correct that these biblical references are anachronistic, what do they show? They need show no more than that the tellers of the patriarchal stories used categories for depicting the patriarchs that were familiar and contemporary to themselves, the storytellers (rather as, say, Rembrandt depicts the patriarchs in the costume and surroundings of the seventeenth century). This is the same phenomenon as that for which I have argued with regard to the use of the divine name YHWH in Genesis 12–50. Although this can be problematic for the modern historical concern that wants to distinguish different historical periods, the merging of historical horizons in traditional storytelling is a readily comprehensible process and is none the worse for representing a practice supposedly uncharacteristic of the modern West.

The whole question of the historical age of the patriarchal world, however, needs to be pressed more closely. For we saw that a story such as ch. 22 stands at such a remove from a second millennium context that one can only be historically agnostic with regard to it. And many scholars are not just agnostic but are thoroughly dismissive about the likelihood of there being any material of genuine antiquity (i.e. the first half of the second millennium) represented in the patriarchal stories. This, therefore, is the issue that must be addressed.

Probably the most obvious argument for the ancient and pre-Yahwistic character of the patriarchal traditions is the number of religious practices to which they refer which are at variance with normative Mosaic Yahwism, especially as this is set out in Deuteronomy. For example, Abraham plants a tree in Beersheba at a place where he worships God (Gen. 21.33), and also builds altars in two places where some special tree already exists (Gen. 12.6-7; 13.18). Yet the law of Deut. 16.21 states, 'You shall not plant any tree as an Asherah beside the altar of YHWH your God which you shall make'. Now of course none of the Genesis passages states that the tree which Abraham planted or beside which he built an altar was an 'Asherah' (a sacred tree or pole, consistently associated in the Old Testament with Canaanite religious practice which is prohibited for Israel, e.g. Judg. 6.25-30; 1 Kgs 14.23; 2 Kgs 18.3-4); nonetheless, it is difficult not to feel that even so there is an obvious affinity between Abraham's practice and that prohibited by Deuteronomy. How then is it that Abraham, the model for Israel's faith, can carry out religious practices forbidden to Israel, yet with no adverse comment from the narrator? The obvious answer would appear to be that the writer takes seriously Abraham's context prior to the giving of Torah to Israel, in which the prohibitions of Deuteronomy simply do not apply because they were not yet given. Similar considerations would apply (a) to the pillar which Jacob sets up at Bethel (Gen. 28.18-22; 35.14-15), against which one could set the prohibition of Deut. 16.22, 'And you shall not set up a pillar, which YHWH your God hates'; or (b) to the fact that Jacob has two wives, Leah and Rachel, and gives preference to the children of his favourite Rachel over the firstborn children of Leah despite the fact that Deut. 21.15-17 explicitly forbids precisely such conduct.

This type of argument was given a completely different slant by Wellhausen in his famous *Prolegomena to the History of Ancient Israel*. Wellhausen's argument is subtle and wide-ranging, but the essential points for our concerns can be stated briefly. Although Wellhausen agreed that much of the religious practice of the patriarchs is at odds with what is prescribed in pentateuchal laws (especially Deuteronomy), he argued that such divergence was not restricted to the patriarchal narratives, but was also characteristic of the narratives in Joshua–2 Kings. For example, Exodus, Leviticus and Numbers envisage the ark as set in the holy of holies where only the high priest may enter once a year (Lev. 16). Yet Samuel, as a young acolyte in the temple at Shiloh, actually sleeps in the place where the ark is (1 Sam. 3.3). Thus the 'abnormalities' of patriarchal religion must be seen as characteristic of early Israelite religion generally.

A major change in Israelite religion came about with Josiah's reform in 621 BC (2 Kgs 22–23) with its attempt to centralize the worship of YHWH in Jerusalem. This was also the period to which Wellhausen ascribed the writing of Deuteronomy; only thereafter were the various practices of earlier religion restricted and proscribed. The result of all this is that patriarchal religious practice is indeed as it is because Torah had not yet been given to prohibit it—but this is simply characteristic of all Israelite religion prior to Josiah's reform. Thus it is not Moses and the origins of Israel that mark the real difference between patriarchal and Mosaic religion, but rather Josiah's reform is the real watershed in Israelite history. Prior to Josiah's reform all Israelite religion was inherently pluralistic and akin to Canaanite religion; after Josiah's reform there began to develop a host of norms to

regulate and distinguish Israel's religion (culminating in the
Priestly legislation—all the laws of Leviticus and Numbers,
and most of the laws of Exodus—of the exilic and post-exilic
period in the late sixth century). Thus the 'abnormal' features
of patriarchal religion are not evidence for anything other
than an origin prior to Josiah's reform. Since, moreover,
Wellhausen considered that all the content of the patriarchal
narratives portrayed conditions which existed in their time of
writing, which were anachronistically retrojected to a much
earlier pre-Israelite period, and that this time of writing was
predominantly the period of prophecy in the eighth and
seventh centuries (the exception being the later Priestly material), so he considered that there was nothing in the patriarchal narratives that was genuinely of the antiquity which
the Pentateuch as it now stands appears to claim for it.

Wellhausen's views about the patriarchal narratives have
been influential but have not as such given rise to a scholarly
consensus, mainly because of a cogent alternative view that
was put forward by A. Alt in his essay, 'The God of the
Fathers'. The basic point on which Alt differed from
Wellhausen was the latter's contention that the content of the
patriarchal stories simply reflected the period of its written
composition, for Alt believed that a long period of oral transmission underlay the written text and had preserved material
that genuinely was of great, and pre-Israelite, antiquity. The
question, of course, is how one can still discern an underlying
oral process, and Alt appealed primarily to two factors; first, a
careful analysis of differences and anomalies within the
written text, which should disclose different levels within it,
and secondly a comparison with an independently attested
religious phenomenon—Nabatean religion in the early centuries AD—which Alt believed to be comparable to patriarchal
religion. What, according to Alt, was attested in Nabatean
inscriptions, and could also be seen in the patriarchal narratives, was a pattern of religion in which an individual had a
personal deity who was the patron of his clan. The essence of
the individual's relation with his deity would centre on the two
things that a person needed most in a nomadic context outside
settled civilization—first, children to continue the clan, and,

secondly, land for the clan to settle in. Since the promise of son and land are both central to the story of Abraham, and since, in particular, they are present in the story of the covenant in Genesis 15, a story with elements 'which give the impression of great antiquity' (p. 65), Alt concluded that here we have genuinely ancient, pre-Israelite, material which was later adopted by Israel into its Yahwistic faith. Although Alt's wide-ranging proposals have been modified in various details by subsequent scholarship, his basic thesis has commanded widespread agreement and has formed the basis of most subsequent accounts of patriarchal religion until very recently.

One important recent development of Alt's work has been made by C. Westermann in his great *Genesis* commentary. Westermann has focused on those elements of patriarchal religion that relate particularly to the familial lifestyle of the patriarchs and the ways in which these differ from the corporate cultic life and worship of Israel. So, for example, he comments that

> The decisive difference between the large-scale cult [sc. of Israel] and that of the patriarchs is that the latter does not construct a domain separated from and independent of ordinary life, but is integrated fully into the life-styles of the small wandering group...Cultic action takes place as part of the life of the group, and arises therefrom; it takes place as required, not because of some cultic prescription (*Genesis 12–36*, pp. 110-11).

Westermann shows how, for example, the places and ways in which the patriarchs worship and offer sacrifice easily fit this basic description.

Once Alt had established the likelihood of the antiquity of at least the core of the patriarchal traditions in terms of their religious practices, further evidence was adduced by W.F. Albright and various other American scholars influenced by him. Here the main concern was to compare the names and customs presented or presupposed in the patriarchal stories with those in texts from elsewhere in the ancient Near East in the second millennium BC, and to argue that the basic similarity of the patriarchal with the extra-biblical material showed that the world portrayed in the patriarchal narratives is genuinely the world of the second millennium. In particular, Mesopotamian texts from Nuzi (fifteenth century BC) have legal material on marriage, adoption and inheritance which offers parallels to patriarchal material. For example, a Nuzi text specifies that a wife, if childless, should provide her husband with a substitute for herself—just as Sarah gave Hagar to Abraham (Gen. 16.1-4). A classic presentation of this approach to the patriarchal stories is that of John Bright in his *History of Israel*. In the third edition of this work (1980), even after taking into account the criticisms of this whole approach (see below), Bright concludes his discussion, 'One's conviction that the patriarchal narratives authentically reflect social customs at home in the second millennium is strengthened' (p. 80).

Although the above position, in stronger or weaker formulations, could be said to have represented a scholarly consensus until quite recently, it does so no longer. The current scholarly mood is not in favour of the antiquity of the patriarchal traditions. Several works in particular have been influential in this regard. First, J. Van Seters, in his *Abraham in History and Tradition*, has attempted to revive what is essentially the position of Wellhausen. He has criticized the view that one can penetrate behind the Genesis text to older, oral traditions, and has argued that the text reflects the period in which it was written, which, in the case of Abraham, he believes to be the Exile in the sixth century. He argues, for example, that 'Ur of the Chaldeans', from which Abraham came (Gen. 11.31; 15.7) would not have been so called before the rise to power of the Chaldeans, i.e. Babylonians, in the late seventh century. This seems a valid point, since elsewhere in the Old Testament the Chaldeans are first mentioned in late seventh-century texts, e.g. Hab 1.6; Jer. 21.4, 9 (although Van Seters does not consider whether this might not be the updating or contemporizing in the sixth century of an older tradition which originally referred just to Ur or qualified it by some other designation of its inhabitants). And he further argues that the tradition of Abraham leaving Ur of the Chaldees, i.e. Babylonia, for Canaan is a coded way of referring to Israel's return from exile in Babylonia to Canaan—a point which depends on the validity of the assumption that the content of the story simply reflects and encodes the concerns of its tellers; although of course an older tradition to this effect would certainly have gained new significance in the exilic period. With regard to the religious practices of the patriarchs, Van Seters argued in a separate article that these simply show the pluralism of Israelite religion prior to Josiah's reform. Although few have been persuaded by Van Seters' own positive proposals, the acuteness with which he has criticized the consensus position has ensured a wide discussion of his views.

A second major contribution is T.L. Thompson's *The Historicity of the Patriarchal Narratives*, which is a critique of the whole approach pioneered and popularized by Albright. Thompson advances two main arguments. First, many of the features of the patriarchal stories which are argued to have second millennium parallels can be found quite as easily to have parallels in the first millennium, and are therefore no proof of antiquity. Secondly, the parallels are much too random, in that they lack chronological precision. If one parallel is from the eighteenth century, another from the fifteenth, and another from the thirteenth, then unless one is willing to discard some of the parallels it is impossible to pin the patriarchal content to a particular period of history, and without some kind of recognizable chronology the material cannot be considered as history.

There are indeed many telling points in Thompson's critique, though it is only decisive against rather simplistic historical claims (which the Albright school on the whole avoided). For if one accepts that the patriarchal traditions have been constantly told and retold, and have incorporated many elements from their retelling, then one would expect the historical sharpness of the traditions to have become more or less blurred. Yet such blurring in no way entails that the origins of the content may not be genuinely ancient. The problem is partly that the nature of the tradition is inherently problematic for the modern historian, and partly that in any case we know so little about the second millennium BC that any historical reconstruction relative to that period must be hypothetical and tentative.

A third major work is the recent German monograph of M. Köckert, *Vätergott und Väterverheissungen*. This is a learned and acute critique of Alt's 'God of the Fathers' and of the whole scholarly consensus (with its various modifications) built upon it. There are perhaps two main elements to Köckert's argument. First, he argues that the patriarchal texts are relatively late (he inclines towards dates in the seventh and sixth centuries) and stand at too great a remove from any supposed patriarchal period. He is sceptical about supposed underlying oral tradition, and emphasizes the primacy of studying the literary processes embodied in the texts as we have them (and it should be noted also that the recent study of P. Kirkpatrick, *The Old Testament and Folklore Study*, denies that oral tradition, if such there was in the patriarchal stories, could have preserved material in recognizable form for even two centuries). Secondly, he argues that many of the supposedly distinctive patriarchal practices are not distinctive at all, but can easily be paralleled from texts of the seventh and sixth centuries. Insofar as there is a distinctive pattern of family-centred religion, this simply shows patterns of family piety that existed within Israel outside the sphere of the official, public cult (i.e. patterns of religion either prior to, or untouched by, Josiah's reform). Thus, with some important modifications, we have a reinstatement of the kind of view of patriarchal religion advocated by Wellhausen.

Although there is much of value in the details of Köckert's analysis, it still leaves important questions unanswered. First, the crucial texts of Exodus 3 and 6, which show Israel's own remarkable awareness of a pre-Yahwistic stage of religion, and which constituted Alt's starting point, receive no discussion by Köckert (or Van Seters or Thompson). Secondly, Köckert gives insufficient attention to basic methodological questions about establishing the dates of texts and their contents. If there are apparent similarities between texts X and Y, this can be explained in a number of ways: X may have influenced Y, Y may have influenced X, both X and Y may have been influenced by Z, the similarities may be accidental, or the similarities may be not be genuine similarities at all.

When Köckert finds apparent similarities between the content of patriarchal stories and that of various seventh and sixth century texts, he rather consistently assumes that the former must be influenced by the latter, or at best be contemporary with it. Yet until all other ways of understanding the relationship have been explored, the kind of conclusion that Köckert draws cannot be considered well founded.

Perhaps what Van Seters, Thompson, and Köckert most clearly show is the difficulty of historical probes into the patriarchal traditions. It becomes extremely difficult, probably impossible, to prove the antiquity of the content of the traditions because of the paucity of evidence and the difficulty of establishing controls. If the patriarchal traditions generally are genuinely ancient but have been subject to retelling and the incorporation of later perspectives—i.e. the stories have become more or less legendary (as defined in Chapter 3 above)—then one would expect them to show similarities to texts which had only originated in later periods. In the last resort, it all seems to depend upon one's educated judgment as to the kind of material that the patriarchal stories should be understood to be (a point well illustrated by W. McKane's *Studies in the Patriarchal Narratives*). As noted above, however, the general scholarly mood at present has moved against the view of the patriarchal stories as legends of genuinely ancient origin, and prefers to see them as largely anachronistic retrojections of writers in the monarchical period. If one examines the most recent textbook history of Israel, J.M. Miller and J.H. Hayes, *A History of Ancient Israel and Judah*, one finds no account of the patriarchal period at all, but only a methodological discussion of the problems of using the patriarchal material as a historical source, with a final reluctance to use it at all.

It can hardly be said that the kind of reconstruction offered by Bright has been refuted in detail, and one's basic approach to the question does seem to be largely a matter of mood. All scholars are aware of the historical difficulties posed by the patriarchal texts; it is just that the Albright–Bright tradition of scholars was confident that at least some of the difficulties could be overcome, while more recent scholars, looking at the same evidence, feel the difficulties to be overwhelming.

A Fresh Approach to the Evidence of Patriarchal Religion

There may be a way forward if, rather than addressing the historical questions about patriarchal religion in their familiar form, one focuses on the question whether or not Israel had a consistent tradition about the nature of patriarchal religion consonant with the belief that the patriarchal period was a time when the name YHWH was not known, a tradition which was maintained by the writers of the patriarchal stories at whatever various historical periods they wrote (see R.W.L. Moberly, *The Old Testament of the Old Testament*, ch. 3). Instead of trying to single out possibly ancient elements (especially name of deity, divine promises), as has been customary since Alt, the aim would be rather to depict a consistent religious ethos which was other than that of Yahwism. A detailed study of the material in this way shows at least seven important and interrelated aspects of patriarchal religion.

First, patriarchal monotheism is open and inclusive. Everyone, including Abimelech of Gerar and Pharaoh in Egypt (Gen. 20, 41), relates to one and the same God, and the notion of a plurality of gods, and the need to choose between them, such as is implied by 'You shall have no other gods before me' (Exod. 20.3), is almost entirely lacking.

Secondly, there is no general antagonism between the patriarchs and the religious practices of the natives of Canaan in the kind of way that frequently recurs in the life of Israel. When Abraham imagines that the inhabitants of Gerar would have no fear of God (20.11), the story explicitly rebuts his assumption (20.4-6). Moreover, although Isaac and Jacob seek wives from Aram rather than Canaan, the reason for this (24.1-9; 27.46–28.9) is never that Canaanite wives would cause them to be religiously unfaithful, as Israel is warned elsewhere (e.g. Exod. 34.11-16).

Thirdly, patriarchal cultic practice is different from that prescribed for Mosaic Yahwism. We have noted earlier the issue of trees and pillars, and one may note also the lack of any sense of prescribed places of worship. There is no hint of the patriarchs observing the sabbath or food laws (which came to the fore at the exile), and even though Abraham is commanded to circumcise his family (Gen. 17), the fact that it is Ishmael whose circumcision is primarily narrated means that circumcision does not carry the significance of exclusive identity that it came to have later.

Fourthly, patriarchal religion is unmediated in that it lacks both prophet and priest. The patriarchs never speak or act on God's behalf in the way that Moses does, nor are they thus spoken to by others; and the patriarchs offer their own sacrifices, without a priest to do it for them. Admittedly, on one occasion Abraham is called a prophet (*nābî'*, 20.7), but this is because he is a man who prays for others, as prophets should (e.g. 1 Sam. 12.19, 23), not because he speaks on God's behalf in characteristic prophetic style; and prayer for others is not intrinsically linked to prophecy.

Fifthly, the patriarchs live in Canaan as sojourners, i.e. temporary residents dependent on others (*gērîm*, e.g. 17.8; 26.3), with no sense that the land really belongs to them or that they ought to fight for it, as is characteristic of Israel. The patriarchs generally maintain a peaceful existence, and when they want land of their own they buy it from its legitimate owners, the Canaanites (23; 33.19).

Sixthly, there is a general lack of moral emphasis in patriarchal religion, which is consistent with its context prior to Sinai and Torah. Promises of blessing are given, without either stipulations of moral obedience or warnings of judgment for disobedience attached to them. The main exception to this is in the stories of Abraham, where the greater moral emphasis (e.g. 17.1; 18.19; 22.12; 26.5) is probably part of the larger appropriation of these stories by Yahwism, with consequent embodiment of Yahwistic emphases (as argued above).

Seventhly, and finally, the generally open, inclusive and unaggressive nature of patriarchal religion is well summed up by its lack of holiness. The language of holiness in the Old Testament is closely connected to the revelation of God as YHWH to Moses and Israel. There is no significant use of the language of holiness anywhere in Genesis 12–50; but as soon as God reveals himself to Moses as YHWH, then for the first time holiness becomes an issue (Exod. 3.5). Although Israel is to be a holy nation set apart for the service of a holy God (Exod. 19)—and with this come all the things that divide Israel from other nations—there is no sense of this in the patriarchal narratives, and that is why their fundamental ethos is distinctive.

What should the historian make of this? A number of points may be made. First, it should be clear that all the above seven points are interrelated and give a recognizable picture of a distinctive religious ethos. Secondly, the ethos of patriarchal religion is clearly other than that of Mosaic Yahwism, certainly as it is presented in the Pentateuch from Exodus to Deuteronomy. Thirdly, it is highly unlikely that such a religious ethos should have been simply invented, least of all by someone who stood within the context of Mosaic Yahwism. If, fourthly, patriarchal religion corresponds to some kind of historical reality, then presumably this is either some form of a genuinely ancient, pre-Yahwistic religion or something that was an 'unorthodox' strand within Yahwistic religion (e.g. prior to Josiah's reform). The difficulty with the latter suggestion is precisely the complete lack of that holiness and exclusiveness which is one of the most fundamental characteristics of Yahwism. It is difficult to imagine any form of Yahwism that did not in some way share these characteristics. The classic move made by Wellhausen and more recent scholars like Van Seters and Köckert to assimilate 'unorthodox' patriarchal religion to 'unorthodox' Yahwism prior to, or outside the context of, Josiah's reform, and simply to see different manifestations of one and the same phenomenon overlooks this one fundamental point. However much religious practice in Joshua–2 Kings is at variance with the prescriptions of pentateuchal law, the basic sense of the religion as committed to YHWH as a holy God is consistent.

In conclusion, therefore, it is probably impossible to prove anything about the historicity of the patriarchal period and patriarchal religion because of the paucity of evidence and controls. This does not mean, however, that a good case cannot be made for supposing that the material is, in its origins, genuinely ancient; it is just that a good case will also be able to be made for the opposite point of view, and no doubt for the next few years it is this that will particularly feature in the literature.

6

AN INVITATION
TO THE IMAGINATION

IT WAS NOTED IN THE FIRST CHAPTER that one of the striking
features of recent Old Testament study has been a widespread
move from reading the text as history to reading it as literature. One of the characteristics of literary approaches is that
they put different questions to the text from those put by the
historian. For example, there is much greater attention to the
patterns and structures of words, and a concern with what
the text as text may mean which is not necessarily identical
with the meaning that its writer intended. One of the pioneering works in this regard was J.P. Fokkelman, *Narrative Art in
Genesis* (1975),the recent reissue of which (1991) presumably
attests its continuing significance. A work which studies the
disposition of key words in the text is A. Abela, *The Themes of
the Abraham Narrative*. And L.A. Turner (*Announcements of
Plot in Genesis*) offers some novel readings of the text by
approaching it as a 'first-time reader', that is, by excluding
from the interpretation all knowledge of developments subsequent to the point in the story under consideration (although
this seems a doubtful method in the light of my fundamental
point that the patriarchal stories are told from, and presuppose, the context of Israel that is subsequent to them).

There is also in many such literary works a greater openness to a use of the imagination (in other than historical ways)
in interpreting the text. Some of the most imaginatively powerful stories, such as Jacob's wrestling at the ford of Jabbok, have
attracted particular attention. For example, a famous

structuralist reading of this story is R. Barthes, 'The Struggle with the Angel'.

Another characteristic of recent study, less widespread but significant nonetheless, has been a renewed interest in the history of interpretation—which generally means a study of pre-modern commentators, who read the text without the historically-minded understanding that has generally characterized biblical study for the last two hundred years. For an example of a detailed study of particular texts, W.T. Miller, *Mysterious Encounters at Mamre and Jabbok*, on the early Jewish and Christian interpretations of Genesis 18 and 32, is full of interesting material.

There has always been some interest in these pre-modern commentators, simply because they constitute part of the history of the discipline. Moreover, for understanding the meaning of difficult Hebrew words and expressions there is a wealth of useful material in mediaeval Jewish commentators, many of whose proposals have been arrived at independently by modern scholars, often unaware of their predecessors. Beyond purely linguistic matters there is much else of interest in pre-modern commentators, although sometimes they have been considered significant primarily insofar as they anticipated something of modern historical insights rather than as being interesting in their own right.

The resurgence of interest in these commentators has not generally been connected explicitly with literary approaches to the text, although sometimes the link is made, as in C. Allen's recent feminist reading of Jacob's deception of Isaac in Genesis 27, 'On Me be the Curse, My Son!' Nonetheless, whether or not the links are made explicit, there is much that is common to the two approaches. For as soon as one ceases to ask the historical questions, and becomes interested in the patterns of the words and their imaginative implications, one may not be doing anything very different from what was done by many pre-modern commentators. It will be appropriate, therefore, in this final chapter to take a few examples from the history of interpretation and to seek to understand how they read the text. This is a study that has both historical and hermeneutical interest.

We shall take examples relating to Genesis 22, since we have already seen how the text may be read from a historically informed perspective, and it will be useful to compare this approach with other readings of the text. Moreover, within the history of Jewish thought and practice the influence of Genesis 22 (which is known as the Akedah, i.e. the 'Binding' [of Isaac]) has been enormous—it has been one of Judaism's key texts, and its significance can hardly be overrated. S. Spiegel (*The Last Trial*) provides a stimulating introduction to the use of Genesis 22 within Judaism, and the recent article of G. Abramson, 'The Reinterpretation of the Akedah in Modern Hebrew Poetry', attests the continuing engagement (albeit often negative and hostile) with Genesis 22 in modern Israel. We shall therefore look first at some examples of Jewish interpretation and only secondarily turn to consider some examples of Christian interpretation.

Jewish Interpretations

1. *The Book of Jubilees*

The *Book of Jubilees* is the oldest extant interpretation of the whole book of Genesis. It is difficult to date precisely, but is probably to be dated about 150 BC. The book is a retelling of the story of Genesis and, much more briefly, of the first half of Exodus until Israel arrives at Mt Sinai to receive the gift of Torah. The story is retold with considerable freedom—when compared with the biblical text—so as to incorporate the perspectives of its teller. Overall, the most striking characteristic is the desire to show that Torah is of eternal validity and so was observed by the patriarchs even before Israel came to Sinai. Thus the distinctiveness of the patriarchal period and religion largely disappears as the material is conformed to the patterns of Torah. For a recent study of this whole topic, see J.C. Endres, *Biblical Interpretation in the Book of Jubilees*.

In the retelling of Genesis 22 there are a number of small differences from the biblical text, and two major differences, one at the beginning and one at the end. It was noted above that there are certain similarities between Genesis 22 and the testing of Job in Job 1–2. These were already appreciated by the writer of *Jubilees*, who expands the brief reference to testing in 22.1 with the more fully developed scenario of Job 1. That is, he introduces the figure of Satan, as the cynic who doubts the genuineness of Abraham's faith, with the result that the test is seen as a demonstration of that genuineness:

> And Prince Mastema [i.e. Satan] came and he said before God, 'Behold, Abraham loves Isaac, his son. And he is more pleased with him than everything. Tell him to offer him (as) a burnt offering upon the altar. And you will see whether he will do this thing. And you will know whether he is faithful in everything in which you test him' (*Jub.* 17.16, trans. O.S. Wintermute, in J.H. Charlesworth [ed.], *The Old Testament Pseudepigrapha*, II, p. 90).

At the climactic moment when God stops Abraham from carrying out the sacrifice and pronounces his assurance about Abraham's fear of God, the text correspondingly inserts the words, 'And Prince Mastema was shamed' (*Jub.* 18.12). This reading of Genesis 22 in the light of Job 1 seems a reasonable imaginative way of trying to understand the text.

The second major addition to the biblical text is at the end, where reference to one of Israel's festivals is introduced. After Abraham returns to Beersheba, we read:

> And he observed this festival every year (for) seven days with rejoicing. And he named it 'the feast of the LORD' according to the seven days during which he went and returned in peace. And thus it is ordained and written in the heavenly tablets concerning Israel and his seed to observe this festival seven days with festal joy (*Jub.* 18.18-19).

The identity of this festival is indicated by a temporal reference at the outset of the story—'in the first month. . . on the twelfth of that month' (*Jub.* 17.15), which, allowing for the fact that Abraham arrived at the place of sacrifice on the third day, means that the story took place on the fourteenth day of the first month, i.e. the day of Passover, which precedes the seven days of unleavened bread (Exod. 12.1-20, esp. vv. 6, 18). This exemplifies the general point made above, about the ascription of what is characteristic of Israel already to the patriarchs. As we have seen that the biblical text itself does this in subtle fashion, by making Abraham a model for Torah obedience, the writer of *Jubilees*, although less subtle than the biblical writer, is doing something perfectly natural for someone operating within a Jewish context that highly esteems obedience to Torah. In hermeneutical terms, this is analogous to the common Christian practice of imaginatively assimilating the stories of the Old Testament to the perspectives and assumptions of Christian theology.

2. *The Commentary of Rashi*
By general consent, the greatest of the mediaeval Jewish commentators was Rashi (an acronym for Rabbi Solomon ben Isaac [in Hebrew, Rabbi Shlomo Yitzhaki]), who lived and worked in France in the eleventh century. He wrote commentaries on both the Bible and the Talmud. Rashi's great strength was that he knew and made use of the great wealth of traditional rabbinic biblical interpretation and at the same time had a sharp eye for the literal and grammatical meaning of the text. (A useful recent introduction to his life and work is C. Pearl, *Rashi*).

Some of Rashi's comments on Genesis 22 are straightforwardly matter-of-fact. He comments on the reference to 'the land of Moriah' in v. 2 by noting that this is Jerusalem and making a cross-reference to the one other mention of Moriah in Scripture, 2 Chron. 3.1, where the identification of Moriah with Jerusalem is explicitly made. Again, when Abraham cuts the wood for the burnt offering (v. 3), Rashi notes that the word for 'cut' in the accompanying targum is also used in 2 Sam. 19.18. For the most part, however, Rashi reads the text imaginatively in the light of general moral and religious concerns.

Rashi's comment on the opening words of Genesis 22 is concerned to illuminate the concept of testing and will be readily understandable in the light of the treatment in *Jubilees*—although he is in fact referring to other texts—and he also gives an additional reason why people took the text in the way they did. For the Hebrew word *dābār*, usually here rendered 'thing' (e.g. 'After these things...') can also mean 'word' (e.g. 'After these words...'). This then raises the question, Which words? So Rashi comments:

Some of our Rabbis say [that it means] after the words of Satan who denounced Abraham saying, 'Of all the banquets which Abraham prepared not a single bullock nor a single ram did he bring as a sacrifice to You'. God replied to him, 'Does he do anything at all except for his son's sake? Yet if I were to bid him, "Sacrifice him to Me", he would not refuse'. Others say [that it means] 'after the words of Ishmael' who boasted to Isaac that he had been circumcised when he was thirteen years old without resisting. Isaac replied to him, 'You think to intimidate me by [mentioning the loss of] one part of the body! If the Holy One, blessed be He, were to tell me, "Sacrifice yourself to Me" I would not refuse' (translation from A.M. Silbermann (ed.), *Pentateuch with Rashi's Commentary: Genesis*, p. 93. Words in square brackets are not in the text but are added to explicate Rashi's concise style of writing).

In v. 2 Rashi notes that Isaac is referred to at some length— 'Take your son, your only son, whom you love, Isaac'. Why should the terms be piled up in this way, especially when one assumes that no word in the Torah is ever wasted? So Rashi imagines a conversation between God and Abraham and comments as follows:

Abraham said [to God], 'I have two sons'. He answered him, 'Thine only son'. Abraham said, 'This one is the only son of his mother and the other is the only son of his mother'. God then said, 'the one whom thou lovest'. Abraham replied, 'I love both of them'. Whereupon God said 'even Isaac'. Why did He not disclose this to him at the very first? So as not to confuse him suddenly lest his mind become distracted and bewildered [and in his confused state he would involuntarily consent, when there would have been no merit in his sacrifice], and so that he might more highly value God's command and that God might reward him for [the increasing sacrifice demanded by obedience to] each and every expression [used here].

One can see that Rashi enters into the world of the text with full imaginative seriousness, and is also seeking to understand developments in such a way that they have paradigmatic moral value.

Other examples of Rashi's close attention to the precise wording are frequent. Given that God intended only to test

Abraham and did not want the actual death of Isaac, Rashi notes that the word in v. 2 $w^eha^a\bar{l}\bar{e}h\hat{u}$, traditionally rendered 'offer [as burnt offering]' may be understood differently, since its literal meaning is 'bring him up/cause him to ascend', and the regular word for 'slaughter/slay [a sacrificial victim]' ($\check{s}\bar{a}\d{h}a\d{t}$) is not used. So Rashi comments:

> He did not say, 'Slay him', because the Holy One, blessed be He, did not desire that he should slay him, but he told him to bring him up to the mountain to prepare him as a burnt offering. So when he had taken him up, God said to him, 'Bring him down'.

Although one may reasonably observe that this is implausible in terms of normal Hebrew idiom—after all, the same phrase used of Isaac in v. 2 is used to describe what actually happened to the ram in v. 13—Rashi's concern is to ask what the text can mean if one is rereading it and looking for possible hints of the eventual denouement. Just the same is Rashi's comment on Abraham's words to his young men in v. 5, 'We will return to you', where he sees significance in the plural verb and comments: 'He prophesied that they would both return'; which, incidentally, appears to be the same reading of the text as in the New Testament, where the plural verb would be the only textual basis for the comment of the writer to the Hebrews that Abraham 'considered that God was able to raise even from the dead' (Heb. 11.19).

Generally speaking, the issue raised by this kind of 'forced' reading of the text concerns the limits to which one may make the meaning of the text as text different from the meaning intended by its author. In general terms, the issue is similar to that raised by much traditional Christian reading of Hebrew Scripture as the Old Testament, where the concern is not necessarily to ask 'What did this originally mean?' but rather 'What does it now mean when it is read in the light of Christ?' The decision whether or not to read a text in the light of its original historical meaning is always a major hermeneutical decision. When the text has to function as scripture for either Jew or Christian, it can be a particularly difficult decision to make.

Christian Interpretations

1. *The Genesis Homilies of Origen*

One of the greatest biblical scholars in the patristic period was
Origen. Writing in the first half of the third century AD,
Origen commented extensively upon both Old and New
Testaments, and was much followed by subsequent commentators. Although he is known particularly for his propensity
for allegory as a way of handling difficulties within the text,
Origen was well aware of the significance of the literal
meaning also. Generally speaking, Origen's work shows a
practical and pastoral concern to read the Old Testament in
the light of Christ and to relate the biblical text to the life of the
Christian community. (A good introduction to his biblical
interpretation is provided by M. Wiles in his article 'Origen as
Biblical Scholar').

Some of Origen's comments on Genesis 22 are those which
almost any reader of the story would make. So, for example,
Origen comments on God's initial command:

> What do you say to these things, Abraham? What kind of
> thoughts are stirring in your heart? A word has been uttered
> by God which is such as to shatter and try your faith. What do
> you say to these things? What are you thinking? What are you
> reconsidering? (translation from R. Heine, *Origen's Homilies
> on Genesis and Exodus*, Homily VIII, 137).

Origen typically answers this rhetorical question not by offering his own speculation but by referring to the New Testament:

> But since 'the spirit of prophets is subject to the prophets'
> [1 Cor. 14.32], the apostle Paul, who, I believe, was teaching
> by the Spirit what feeling, what plan Abraham considered,
> has revealed it when he says: 'By faith Abraham did not hesi-
> tate, when he offered his only son, in whom he had received
> the promises, thinking that God is able to raise him up even
> from the dead' [Heb. 11.17, 19] (*ibid.*).

From this Origen deduces that 'the faith in the resurrection
began to be held already at that time in Isaac'. This interpretation in the letter to the Hebrews is particularly important for
Origen, for he makes use of it again in commenting on
Abraham's words to his servants that 'we will return' (v. 5):

> Tell me, Abraham, are you saying to the servants in truth
> that you will worship and return with the child, or are you
> deceiving them? If you are telling the truth, then you will not
> make him a holocaust. If you are deceiving, it is not fitting
> for so great a patriarch to deceive. What disposition, there-
> fore, does this statment indicate in you? I am speaking the
> truth, he says, and I offer the child as a holocaust. For for
> this reason I both carry wood with me, and I return to you
> with him. For I believe, and this is my faith, that 'God is able
> to raise him up even from the dead' (p. 140).

Although in these ways Origen engages closely with the question of the literal meaning of the text (when read in the light of
the New Testament), he also handles the text more freely and
introduces typology where appropriate:

> That Isaac himself carries on himself 'the wood for the holo-
> caust' is a figure, because Christ also 'himself carried his
> own cross' [cf. Jn 19.17], and yet to carry 'the wood for the
> holocaust' is the duty of a priest. He himself, therefore,
> becomes both victim and priest (pp. 140-41).

Since Origen considers that the ram which Abraham offers in
sacrifice also represents Christ, this raises a problem of double
typology, the problem of how 'both are appropriate to Christ,
both Isaac who is not slain and the ram which is slain'. This
leads Origen into a discussion, which to most modern readers
seems far-fetched, of how the ram represents Christ in the
flesh (in which Christ suffered and died, and also was a victim)
while Isaac represents Christ in the spirit (in which also he is
a priest).

It will be appropriate to conclude our extracts from Origen
with two of his comments on Gen. 22.12. First, Origen picks up
a problem that has puzzled many a reader:

> In this statement it is usually thrown out against us that God
> says that now he had learned that Abraham fears God as
> though he were such as not to have known previously. God
> knew and it was not hidden from him, since it is he 'who has
> known all things before they come to pass' [Dan. 13.42, the
> story of Susanna]. But these things are written on account of
> you, because you too indeed have believed in God, but unless
> you shall fulfil 'the works of faith' [cf. 2 Thess. 1.11], unless
> you shall be obedient to all the commands, even the more

difficult ones, unless you shall offer sacrifice and show that
you place neither father nor mother nor sons before God [cf.
Matt. 10.37], you will not know that you fear God nor will it be
said of you: 'Now I know that you fear God' (p. 143).

Secondly, Origen uses Paul's apparent reference to Genesis 22
to draw a classic Christian moral from the story, where the
typology is at its loosest:

But grant that these words are spoken to Abraham and he is
said to fear God. Why? Because he did not spare his son. But
let us compare these words with those of the Apostle, where
he says of God: 'Who spared not his own son, but delivered
him up for us all' [Rom. 8.32]. Behold God contending with
men in magnificent liberality: Abraham offered God a mortal
son who was not put to death; God delivered to death an
immortal son for men (p. 144).

2. *The Commentary of Gerhard von Rad*

The German scholar G. von Rad is widely recognized as the
outstanding Christian commentator on the Old Testament in
the twentieth century. Von Rad's work has proved both seminal and controversial for Old Testament study over the last 50
years. Even his critics generally concede that his reading of
the biblical text is marked by unusual freshness and perspica-
city. A useful introduction to his life and work is J.L. Crenshaw,
Gerhard von Rad.

One of the reasons why von Rad's work is controversial is
that basic methodological questions of precisely what it is that
he is doing are not always satisfactorily resolved. That is,
much of the time von Rad is working essentially as a religious
historian, producing descriptive historical accounts of the
religious thought of ancient Israel. Yet sometimes he works as
a Christian theologian, writing from the explicit perspective of
Christian faith and seeking to produce constructive theology,
relevant to the life of the Church. Although these two tasks
need not be incompatible, the relationship between them
sometimes seems unclear in von Rad's work.

In his *Genesis* commentary von Rad makes clear that his
primary task is to interpret the text as a Christian theologian.
For he concludes his introduction by saying:

We receive the Old Testament from the hands of Jesus Christ, and therefore all exegesis of the Old Testament depends on whom one thinks Jesus Christ to be...in the patriarchal narratives, which know so well how God can conceal himself, we see a revelation of God which precedes his manifestation in Jesus Christ. What we are told here of the trials of a God who hides himself and whose promise is delayed, and yet of his comfort and support, can readily be read into God's revelation of himself in Jesus Christ (*Genesis*, p. 43).

This means that von Rad is identifying himself with the historic Christian appropriation of the Old Testament as Christian Scripture, in which the interpreter's starting-point is a Christological understanding of God and faith. This must necessarily mean that in reading the Old Testament the concern cannot be solely the historian's question of 'What did this text originally mean?' but rather 'What does this text now mean when it is read in the light of Christ?' Given the predominance of the historian's agenda in modern Old Testament interpretation, it is hardly surprising that this theological agenda of von Rad has proved controversial.

When we come to Genesis 22, both the strengths and the weaknesses of von Rad's approach can be seen. The key passages of von Rad's interpretation of the story are as follows:

One must indeed speak of a temptation *(Anfechtung)* which came upon Abraham but only in the definite sense that it came from God only, the God of Israel...For Abraham, God's command is completely incomprehensible...Isaac is the child of promise. In him every saving thing that God has promised to do is invested and guaranteed. The point here is not a natural gift, not even the highest, but rather the disappearance from Abraham's life of the whole promise. Therefore, unfortunately, one can only answer all plaintive scruples about this narrative by saying that it concerns something much more frightful than child sacrifice. It has to do with a road out into Godforsakenness *(Gottverlassenheit)*, a road on which Abraham does not know that God is only testing him...In this test God confronts Abraham with the question whether he could give up God's gift of promise. He had to be able (and he was able), for it is not a good that may be retained by virtue of any legal title or with the help of a

human demand. God therefore poses before Abraham the
question whether he really understands the gift of promise as
a pure gift (*Genesis*, pp. 239, 244).

A few comments may help elucidate the significance of what
von Rad is saying. First, von Rad was a Lutheran, and at the
heart of Lutheran theology stands a theology of the cross, an
understanding of God and life in the light of Jesus' cry of
dereliction in Matthew and Mark's account of the crucifixion
—'My God, my God, why have you forsaken (*verlassen*) me?'
So when Abraham is on a road out into Godforsakenness, his
story is being understood by analogy with the crucifixion of
Christ.

Secondly, Luther's theology of the cross revolves around two
key concepts. On the one hand, the hiddenness of God. For the
true revelation of God comes in the cross where God is hidden
and so can only be perceived by the eye of faith. This is why for
Abraham God's command is incomprehensible and has to be
received by faith. On the other hand, *Anfechtung*. This is an
impossible word to render in English, but it may perhaps be
represented by terms such as affliction, anguish, temptation.
What it means is that God works in people by breaking them
down, stripping away all customary supports and comforts,
and bringing them through suffering to a true recognition of
God as he really is. So when von Rad interprets God's testing of
Abraham as *Anfechtung*, it is this kind of spiritual process that
he is depicting, understood again by analogy with the cross.

In conclusion, three comments may be made. First, von
Rad's interpretation is a sophisticated Christian typology. He
reads the story of Abraham in the light of Christ and Christian
theology, and so presents the story of Abraham as a type of
Christ's suffering on the cross. As such von Rad stands in a
real continuity with classical Christian commentators, from
the Fathers onwards, and well illustrates the way in which
the Old Testament, as Christian Scripture, is *not* read 'like
any other book'.

Secondly, although von Rad's interpretation gives a quite
different meaning to the story from that which I suggested it
had in its Old Testament context, nonetheless there is a real
sense in which von Rad is doing the same kind of thing that

the ancient Hebrew writer of Genesis 22 was doing. For we saw that the Hebrew writer interpreted what was originally non-Yahwistic material from the perspective of Yahwism. In doing so the writer assimilated the story to the central theological concerns of Yahwism, particularly obedience to Torah. Von Rad has read what was originally a non-Christian story from the perspective of Christianity, and in so doing has assimilated the story to the central theological concerns of Lutheranism. The hermeneutical assumptions at stake are similar, and the difference in result is the difference in the theological content of the interpreter's standpoint.

Finally, by what yardstick should von Rad's interpretation be assessed? If it is assessed in terms of its conformity to the originally intended meaning of the Hebrew text, then it does not fare very well. A story of Abraham suffering from *Anfechtung* and Godforsakenness is a considerable way from a story of Abraham being shown to be a model for Israel of Torah obedience at Jerusalem. The strength of von Rad's reading is twofold. On the one hand, it is imaginatively powerful, and has the same validity as any literary creation that manages to capture the imagination. On the other hand, it is in conformity with the norms of the Christian community from which, and for which, von Rad writes. Ultimately, it is likely to be one's stance towards that community which determines one's assessment of the interpretation. As noted at the beginning of the book, the question of what counts as a good reading of the biblical text cannot be divorced from questions about the context and interpretative community within which the reader stands.

Further Reading

Commentaries

Brueggemann, W., *Genesis* (IBC; Atlanta: John Knox, 1982). Aimed at preachers. Brueggemann discusses the text from the perspective of Christian theology.

Coats, G.W., *Genesis, with an Introduction to Narrative Literature* (FOTL, 1; Grand Rapids: Eerdmans, 1983). Some useful analyses of the text.

Delitzsch, F., *A New Commentary on Genesis* (2 vols.; Edinburgh: T. & T. Clark, 1888–89). Dated, but still an instructive engagement with the text, with much discussion of Hebrew.

Driver, S.R., *The Book of Genesis* (London: Methuen, 4th edn, 1905). The standard commentary in English for many years in the earlier part of this century, it went through many editions. Although dated, still a first-rate exposition of an older critical consensus.

Gunkel, H., *Genesis* (HKAT; Göttingen: Vandenhoeck & Ruprecht, 5th edn, 1922; reprinted in 1964 as '6th edn'). Probably the most influential Genesis commentary of the twentieth century; unfortunately never translated into English.

Kidner, F.D., *Genesis* (TOTC; London: Tyndale Press, 1967). Brief, but with many sharp insights. Kidner eschews most modern perspectives on historical and compositional issues.

Plaut, W.G. (ed.), *The Torah: A Modern Commentary* (New York: Union of American Hebrew Congregations, 1981), pp. 87-360. With Hebrew text and translation. A useful combination of traditional Jewish and modern perspectives.

Rad, G. von, *Genesis* (OTL; London: SCM Press, 1972 [ET from the 9th German edn, Göttingen: Vandenhoeck & Ruprecht, 1972]). The outstanding modern theological commentary.

Sarna, N.M., *Bereishith/Genesis* (JPS Torah Commentary; Philadelphia: Jewish Publication Society, 5749/1989). With Hebrew text and translation. An attractive combination of traditional Jewish perspectives with sober use of modern critical insight.

Scherman, N., and M. Zlotowitz (eds.), *Bereishis/Genesis: A New Translation with a Commentary Anthologized from Talmudic, Midrashic and Rabbinic Sources* (Artscroll Tanach Series; 2 vols.; Brooklyn, NY: Mesorah Publications, 1986 [originally in 6 separate vols., 1977–82]). A valuable extensive compilation of traditional Jewish insights, but with no concessions at all to any modern insights.

Skinner, J., *Genesis* (ICC; Edinburgh: T. & T. Clark, 1912). Dated, but, like all ICC volumes, packed with useful information especially on historical and linguistic matters.

Speiser, E., *Genesis* (AB; Garden City, NY: Doubleday, 1964). Useful for wider historical background, but otherwise thin.

Vawter, B., *On Genesis: A New Reading* (London: Geoffrey Chapman, 1977). The reading is less new than the title suggests and represents a consensus approach.

Wenham, G.J., *Genesis 1–15* (WBC, 1; Waco, TX: Word Books, 1987). Probably the most useful commentary for the beginner in Hebrew, since all possibly difficult Hebrew words are parsed and there is discussion of Hebrew usage. The second volume, on Genesis 16–50, should be appearing shortly.

Westermann, C., *Genesis 12–36* (London: SPCK, 1986 [ET from the German edn, Neukirchen–Vluyn: Neukirchener Verlag, 1981]). The most exhaustive modern commentary, indispensable for serious study, although somewhat thin on theology.

—*Genesis 37–50* (London: SPCK, 1987 [ET from the German edn, Neukirchen–Vluyn: Neukirchener Verlag, 1982]).

—*Genesis: A Practical Commentary* (Grand Rapids: Eerdmans, 1987). A popularly oriented condensation of his major commentary.

Works Referred to in the Text

Abela, A., *The Themes of the Abraham Narrative* (Malta: Studia Editions, 1989). A literary discussion of key words and motifs.

Abramson, G., 'The Reinterpretation of the Akedah in Modern Hebrew Poetry', *JJS* 41 (1990), pp. 101-14. Abramson discusses the impact of Genesis 22 in modern Israeli literature.

Allen, C.G., 'On Me be the Curse, My Son!', in R.M. Gross (ed.), *Beyond Androcentrism: New Essays on Women and Religion* (Missoula, MT: Scholars Press, 1977), pp. 183-216, revised in M.J. Buss (ed.), *Encounter with the Text: Form and History in the Hebrew Bible* (Missoula, MT: Scholars Press, 1979), pp. 159-72. A feminist reading of Genesis 27 that draws on pre-modern interpretations.

Alt, A., 'The God of the Fathers', in his *Essays on Old Testament History and Religion* (The Biblical Seminar; Sheffield: JSOT Press, 1989 [ET from the German edn of 1929]), pp. 1-77. Alt set the agenda for subsequent study of patriarchal religion.

Alter, R., *The Art of Biblical Narrative* (London: George Allen & Unwin, 1981). A stimulating and creative literary approach.

Auerbach, E., *Mimesis* (Princeton: Princeton University Press, 1968 [1953]), ch. 1. A classic literary analysis of Genesis 22, in which the storytelling style of Genesis is compared with that of Homer.

Barthes, R., 'The Struggle with the Angel: Textual Analysis of Genesis 32.22-32', in his *Image–Music–Text* (London: Flamingo, 1984), pp. 125-41 (translated from *Analyse structurale et exégèse biblique* [Neuchâtel, 1971]). A famous structuralist reading.

Blum, E., *Die Komposition der Vätergeschichte* (WMANT, 57; Neukirchen–

Vluyn: Neukirchener Verlag, 1984). Blum develops the new look on pentateuchal criticism advocated by Rendtorff.

Bright, J., *A History of Israel* (OTL; London: SCM Press, 3rd edn, 1981). A standard textbook for a number of years.

Charlesworth, J.H., *The Old Testament Pseudepigrapha*, II (London: Darton, Longman & Todd, 1985). This volume contains, among other things, an annotated translation of the *Book of Jubilees* by O.S. Wintermute.

Crenshaw, J.L., *Gerhard von Rad* (Makers of the Modern Theological Mind; Waco, TX: Word Books, 1978). An introduction to von Rad's life and work.

Driver, S.R., *Introduction to the Literature of the Old Testament* (Edinburgh: T. & T. Clark, 6th edn, 1897). For many years a standard exposition of a modern critical approach.

Emerton, J.A., 'Wisdom', in G.W. Anderson (ed.), *Tradition and Interpretation* (Oxford: Clarendon Press, 1979), pp. 214-37. Emerton surveys the debate about wisdom literature, including reference to the Joseph story.

Endres, J.C., *Biblical Interpretation in the Book of Jubilees* (CBQMS, 18; Washington, DC: Catholic Biblical Association, 1987). A recent study of early biblical hermeneutics.

Fokkelman, J.P., *Narrative Art in Genesis* (The Biblical Seminar; Sheffield: JSOT Press, 2nd edn, 1991 [orig. pub. Assen: van Gorcum, 1975]). A controversial pioneering literary study of selected stories.

Gottwald, N.K., *The Hebrew Bible: A Socio-Literary Introduction* (Philadelphia: Fortress Press, 1985).

Gunn, D.M., 'New Directions in the Study of Hebrew Narrative', *JSOT* 39 (1987), pp. 65-75. Gunn discusses the shift from historical to literary approaches to the text.

Hals, R.M., 'Legend', *CBQ* 34 (1972), pp. 166-76; repr. in G.W. Coats (ed.), *Saga, Legend, Tale, Novella, Fable* (JSOTSup, 35; Sheffield: JSOT Press, 1985). A helpful discussion of the varied uses of 'legend'.

Heine, R. (ed.), *Origen's Homilies on Genesis and Exodus* (Fathers of the Church, 71; Washington, DC: Catholic University of America, 1982).

Hendel, R.S., *The Epic of the Patriarch: The Jacob Cycle and the Narrative Traditions of Canaan and Israel* (HSM, 42; Atlanta: Scholars Press, 1987). Chapter 1 offers a useful survey of the history of modern interpretation of the Jacob material.

Humphreys, W. Lee, 'A Life Style for Diaspora: A Study of the Tales of Esther and Daniel', *JBL* 92 (1973), pp. 211-23. Humphries notes links of the Joseph story with Esther and Daniel.

Jowett, B., 'On the Interpretation of Scripture', in *Essays and Reviews* (London: Longman, 1860), pp. 330-433. Page 338 has the famous proposal to 'read Scripture like any other book'.

Kirkpatrick, P.G., *The Old Testament and Folklore Study* (JSOTSup, 62; Sheffield: JSOT Press, 1988). Kirkpatrick doubts whether oral tradition can preserve an accurate account of events.

Koch, K., *The Growth of the Biblical Tradition: The Form-Critical Method*

(London: A. & C. Black, 1969 [ET from the German edn of 1964, 1967]), pp. 111-32. An extensive source-critical and traditio-historical study of Gen. 12.10-20, 20.1-18 and 26.5-11.

Köckert, M., *Vätergott und Väterverheissungen* (FRLANT, 142; Göttingen: Vandenhoeck & Ruprecht, 1988). Köckert criticizes the consensus view of patriarchal religion built upon the work of Alt.

Lemche, N.P., *Ancient Israel: A New History of Israelite Society* (The Biblical Seminar; Sheffield: JSOT Press, 1988). Lemche proposes a view of Israel's history that departs radically from the outlines of the Old Testament.

McKane, W., *Studies in the Patriarchal Narratives* (Edinburgh: Handsel, 1979). Focusing on traditio-historical study, McKane shows how purported development of the tradition varies according to the literary type assigned to the material.

Magonet, J., *A Rabbi's Bible* (London: SCM Press, 1991). An entertaining approach to the problems of biblical interpretation from a Jewish perspective.

Mann, T.W., *The Book of the Torah: The Narrative Integrity of the Pentateuch* (Atlanta: John Knox, 1988), pp. 29-77. A sophisticated reading of Genesis 12–50.

Mare, W. Harold, *The Archaeology of the Jerusalem Area* (Grand Rapids: Baker, 1987).

Miller, J.M., and J.H. Hayes, *A History of Ancient Israel and Judah* (London: SCM Press, 1986), ch. 2. Miller focuses on methodological problems involved in any historical work on Genesis 12–50.

Miller, W.T., *Mysterious Encounters at Mamre and Jabbok* (BJS; Chico, CA: Scholars Press, 1984). Useful for its discussion of early Jewish and Christian interpretations of Genesis 18 and 32.

Moberly, R.W.L., 'The Earliest Commentary on the Akedah', *VT* 38 (1988), pp. 302-23. A study of Gen. 22.15-18.

—*The Old Testament of the Old Testament* (Overtures to Biblical Theology; Philadelphia: Augsburg–Fortress, 1992). The thesis of this book is that Genesis 12–50 stands in relation to the Mosaic Yahwism of Exodus 3 onwards as a kind of Old Testament.

Noth, M., *A History of Pentateuchal Traditions* (Chico, CA: Scholars Press, 1981 [ET from German]). The major modern traditio-historical study of the Pentateuch.

Otto, R., *The Idea of the Holy* (London: Oxford University Press, 1924 [ET from German]). A classic modern study.

Pearl, C., *Rashi* (Jewish Thinkers; London: Weidenfeld & Nicolson, 1988). An introduction to Rashi's life and work.

Pritchard, J.B., *Ancient Near Eastern Texts Relating to the Old Testament* (Princeton: Princeton University Press, 1969). The standard modern edition.

Rad, G. von, 'The Form-Critical Problem of the Hexateuch', in *idem, The Problem of the Hexateuch*, pp. 1-78. This essay proposed fresh categories for Pentateuchal criticism.

—'The Beginnings of Historical Writing in Ancient Israel', in *idem, The*

Problem of the Hexateuch, pp. 166-204 (ET from the German edn of 1944). Von Rad argued in this essay for a change in Israelite writing during the 'Solomonic Enlightenment'.

—'The Joseph Narrative and Ancient Wisdom', in *idem*, *The Problem of the Hexateuch*, pp. 292-300 (originally in *VTS* 1 [1953], pp. 120-27). A ground-breaking proposal to interpret the Joseph story in the categories of the wisdom literature.

—*The Problem of the Hexateuch and Other Essays* (London: SCM Press, 1984).

Rendtorff, R., *The Problem of the Process of Transmission in the Pentateuch* (JSOTSup, 89; Sheffield: JSOT Press, 1990 [ET from the German edn of 1977]). This work helped bring about a rethinking of pentateuchal criticism.

Silbermann, A.M., *Pentateuch with Rashi's Commentary: Genesis* (Jerusalem: Silbermann, 5733/1972). With text, translation and notes of the great Jewish commentator.

Soggin, J.A., *A History of Israel* (London: SCM Press, 1984 [ET from the Italian edn of 1985]), pp. 89-108. A cautious survey of recent debate.

Spiegel, S., *The Last Trial* (New York: Behrman House, 1979). An introduction to history of Jewish interpretation of Genesis 22.

Sternberg, M., *The Poetics of Biblical Narrative: Ideological Literature and the Drama of Reading* (Bloomington, IN: Indiana University Press, 1985). A demanding but worthwhile literary approach. The first three chapters give the essence of the approach advocated.

Thompson, R.J., *Moses and the Law in a Century of Criticism since Graf* (VTSup, 19; Leiden: Brill, 1970). A useful survey of the development of modern pentateuchal criticism.

Thompson, T.L., *The Historicity of the Patriarchal Narratives* (BZAW, 133; Berlin: de Gruyter, 1974). Thompson criticizes the consensus view of the Albright school.

Trible, P., *Texts of Terror: Literary-Feminist Readings of Biblical Narratives* (Overtures to Biblical Theology; Philadelphia: Fortress Press, 1984). Chapter 1 offers a close reading of the story of Hagar in Genesis 16 and 21.

Turner, L.A., *Announcements of Plot in Genesis* (JSOTSup, 96; Sheffield: JSOT Press, 1990). A literary analysis from the perspective of the 'first-time reader'.

Van Seters, J., *Abraham in History and Tradition* (New Haven: Yale University Press, 1975). Van Seters criticizes conventional views of pentateuchal criticism.

—'The Religion of the Patriarchs in Genesis', *Bib* 61 (1980), pp. 220-33. An argument against the supposed antiquity of patriarchal religion.

Weiser, A., *Introduction to the Old Testament* (London: Darton, Longman & Todd, 1961 [ET from German]).

Wellhausen, J., *Prolegomena to the History of Ancient Israel* (Gloucester, MA: Peter Smith, 1973 [repr. from German]). The work that fixed the categories for modern pentateuchal criticism.

—*Die Composition des Hexateuchs und der Historischen Bücher des Alten*

Testaments (Berlin: Georg Reimer, 3rd edn, 1899). This work provides the detailed analysis underlying the documentary hypothesis.

Whybray, R.N., *The Making of the Pentateuch: A Methodological Study* (JSOTSup, 53; Sheffield: JSOT Press, 1987). The most telling critique of the documentary hypothesis, although it deals only with narrative and not with law and is weak on positive alternatives.

Wiles, M.F., 'Origen as Biblical Scholar', in P.R. Ackroyd and C.F. Evans (eds.), *The Cambridge History of the Bible* (Cambridge: Cambridge University Press, 1970), I, pp. 454-89. A useful introduction to one of the great patristic biblical scholars.

Winton Thomas, D., *Documents from Old Testament Times* (New York: Harper & Row, 1961). A useful collection, more condensed than Pritchard.

INDEX OF BIBLICAL REFERENCES

OLD TESTAMENT

INDEX OF AUTHORS